How to Meditate

Using

Chakras, Mantras, and Breath

How to Meditate

Using

Chakras, Mantras, and Breath

Dennis K. Chernin, M.D., M.P.H.

Think Publishing, L.L.C.
Ann Arbor, Michigan

Library of Congress Control Number: 2001119031
How to Meditate Using Chakras, Mantras, and Breath
by Dennis K. Chernin
1. Meditation. 2. Spirituality. 3. Health.

ISBN 0-9714558-0-5 (Paperback book)
ISBN 0-9714558-1-3 (Paperback book with audio CDs)

First edition 2001   Second edition (revised) 2002
Third edition 2003   Fourth edition 2006
10 9 8 7 6 5 4

Published by:
Think Publishing L.L.C.
2345 S. Huron Parkway
Ann Arbor, Michigan 48104
Tel.734-973-3030   Fax 734-973-3057

dennischernin@hotmail.com (to order)
www.dennischernin.com (to order and information on classes)

Printed by:
Cushing-Malloy
Ann Arbor, Mi., USA

Book cover and illustrations done by Jim Horton, Steven Hixon

Layout formatting by Richard Bowman

Edited by Mary Gillis

Contents

Preface

My spiritual journey on the path of meditation began without conscious awareness. While in elementary school, I had incapacitating dizzy spells. At night, alone in my room, I desperately sought ways to make the world stop spinning. Automatically and somewhat inexplicably, I found myself regulating the inflow and outflow of my breath. As I focused on my breathing, I felt calmer, less anxious, and to my great relief, the dreaded vertigo would slowly stop. Intuitively, I sensed that there was great power in this type of concentration, but it would be several years before I would really understand why.

Like many people in the '60s and '70s, I was introduced to the practice and theory of meditation through the books written by Alan Watts on Zen Buddhism and Eastern philosophy and the book *Autobiography of a Yogi* written by Paramahansa Yogananda. The ongoing traumas of the Vietnam War and a changing spiritual milieu in the United States also led many of us to look for higher meaning and truth. During college at Northwestern University in the late '60s and in medical school at the University of Michigan in the early '70s, I explored several different approaches to meditation, including Zen and Tibetan Buddhism as well as Taoism and tai chi. Being Jewish, I also explored meditative approaches and more spiritually based practices of Judaism.

I found that the great philosophies and traditions of India particularly inspired me intellectually and pragmatically. There, the techniques of meditation were presented in a concise, systematic, and thorough way. During my psychiatry residency at the University of Wisconsin in Madison, I studied with Swami Ajaya, a Western-born psychologist who wrote a clear and practical guide for meditation called *Yoga Psychology*. Later, in 1976, I met his teacher, Swami Rama, who was the spiritual guide of the Himalayan Institute. I was particularly interested in his scientific approach to meditation and how he had learned to exert great control over normally involuntary mental and physical functions.

My wife, Jan, and I intensively studied meditation (as well as alternative and holistic medicine) with Swami Rama for several years near Chicago, Illinois. Swami Rama, who died in 1996, was an enigmatic and charismatic man who had great depth of knowledge and personal experience with meditation, which he readily shared with his students. Through my association with the Himalayan Institute, I learned that the knowledge gained from meditation and the power and influence derived from being a teacher of meditation need to be harnessed and directed carefully. I also learned that it is essential to trust one's own inner meditation practice and not depend too heavily on the teacher as the most important guide to spiritual growth.

The techniques that Swami Rama imparted to Jan and me are the same practices that form the basis of my meditation today. This meditative tradition is based on the Eastern philosophies of Vedanta, Samkhya, and Tantra and has been continuously handed down from teacher to student for thousands of years. I have personally practiced all the techniques presented in these pages and have thoroughly studied the theory behind them. Zen and Tibetan Buddhist philosophy and psychology have also influenced my meditation practice, especially in the application of mindfulness, compassion, and simplicity to everyday life. While in my own practice I often incorporate several Jewish meditation techniques, I have not discussed these in much depth in this book because they are associated with a specific religious tradition. The techniques associated with the above-mentioned Eastern traditions are universal and anyone can practice them, whether or not they follow a specific religion.

****

Meditation has been a source of inspiration and comfort for me over the years. Our common interest in meditation philosophy and practice has always been important for Jan and me. I have experienced the wonders of the birth and growth of my children, Abe, Ethan, and Ari and meditation has helped me stay focused and present, always trying to provide them with love and moral guidance. After the death of our son Nathaniel in 1981 to SIDS, meditation gave me moments of refuge and peace during those sad, dark early days.

I have experienced periods when my meditation seemed stagnant and also have had moments of great inspiration and creative insight. I have had experiences when my body would spontaneously assume different yoga postures and other times when I would automatically do advanced breathing exercises, indicating the activation and release of inner, latent energy within my body. I have also had visual and auditory experiences that I can only describe as inspiring, joyful, and at times blissful. I have also had to face conscious and unconscious anxieties and fears that sometimes arise during meditation. I have been consistent with my practice at times and have gotten discouraged or lazy and avoided meditation on occasion. Through it all, meditation has provided me with strength and courage to understand my past, enjoy the present, and prepare for the future.

There are several important people in my life who have closely shared my journey on the path of meditation. My wife, Jan, consistently loves and encourages me and, at the same time, perceptively reminds me to check my ego at the door. Our children, Abe, Ethan, and Ari, are wonderful people whom I love dearly and who inspire me to be the best man I can be. My father, Jack, who recently passed away, and his wife, Jackie, have always loved and supported me even when our earlier ashram life seemed a bit strange to them.

Rosanne Emanuele has been a close and valued friend and we have shared many hours discussing the intricacies and obstacles in our practices. My childhood friend, Rick Frires, M.D., continues to be a close and important confidant and we always enjoy comparing notes on our long and intersecting spiritual paths. In

1998 Jan and I traveled to India where we taught meditation and holistic approaches to health care at a new medical school located in the foothills of the Himalayas, called the Himalayan Institute Hospital Trust. This was our first time in India and we found the experience inspiring and exhilarating. Here, we enjoyed meeting up with Barb Bova, a homeopath and old friend from the Himalayan Institute, whose devotion to yogic practice and healing closely parallels our paths.

I would also like to acknowledge several people who assisted me in writing this book. I greatly appreciate the editorial help of Mary Gillis. Her careful, thoughtful, and critical perspectives were very important, especially in the areas of organization, style, and grammar. Jim Horton did a fine job on the illustrations. We spent many hours trying to get the *chakra* colors and geometric shapes precise. Pat Young, fellow soccer and baseball coach, was very helpful in solving some technical problems with the computer graphics. Steven Hixon redesigned the cover for the second edition and did a wonderful job. Carol Karr has developed a colorful and dynamic web site for my book and medical practice and has given me good advice on marketing.

I greatly appreciate the help of my friend Muruga Booker who used his extraordinary drumming and musical skills to enhance the two guided meditation CDs that accompany this book. My lawyer and Qi Gong healer-colleague, Marty Kriegel, and I have shared many books, laughs, and abstract late-night discussions on the theory and practice of meditation. Marty helped me with several ideas especially the organizational structure of chapter 24, The Technique of Meditation. I also appreciate the help and support of my sister, Donna Chernin Kurit, a long-time professional journalist, who gave me several good suggestions in writing style and also provided some needed editorial insight.

Since I first published my book, I have become good friends with James Arond-Thomas, MD, a holistically oriented oncologist and pharmacologist. He and I have collaborated on writing and lecturing on meditation and hope to write a book together on the interface between meditation, DNA, the cell, and consciousness. I would also like to thank my good friend and colleague, Greg Manteuffel, M.D. who encouraged me to adapt and use several ideas we developed and documented in our book written in 1984 called *Health: A Holistic Approach*.

****

I actually began writing this book by chance. While doing research for a meditation class I was teaching in the fall of 2000, I found there was quite a lot of information on meditation. I discovered, however, that the books written were often incomplete, used too much Sanskrit in their descriptions, or were not systematic enough in the practices of meditation. Often the actual techniques of meditation were not described in enough detail, leaving the reader with some theory but without the practical tools to establish a practice. For these reasons, I decided to write this book, detailing the meditation I use in my own practice, as well as teach to my students. I hope readers find this information useful in helping to understand the theory and principles of meditation and as a systematic guide to establishing a consistent and deep meditation practice.

Introduction

I have written this book to help students understand the theory of meditation as well as to establish a systematic and precise meditation practice. I wanted to share specific concepts and techniques I have studied, practiced, and enjoyed over the years. Because I offer both individualized instruction on meditation and breathing techniques in my medical practice as well as teach larger classes and seminars, I also wanted to address many of the thought-provoking questions asked by my students, patients, colleagues, and friends in these settings.

This book can be used by both beginning students and by individuals who have had experience with meditation and breathing techniques and would like to refine or deepen their practice. People with specific physical illnesses or mental health concerns can also use this book if they are interested in using meditation and breathing techniques as part of their treatment plan. Needless to say, individuals with more serious health problems should consult a health care provider before attempting these practices.

In order to meet the aforementioned goals, I have organized this book into five parts. The meditation technique that I practice and teach is presented in detail in Part V. Accompanying tapes or audio CDs that systematically lead the practitioner through various phases of the meditation can be used in conjunction with or separately from this book.

Part I is called What Is Meditation? In the first chapter, meditation is defined as sustained and uninterrupted concentration on a single object. Next, there is an overview of the goals of meditation. We explore the question of why we practice meditation, and look at what it means to attain expanded states of consciousness. Different forms of meditation are described from both Eastern and Western perspectives. Misconceptions about meditation are clarified, and there is a discussion of the differences between meditation and concentration, contemplation, and prayer.

Next, we explore emotional, psychological, and spiritual benefits of meditation as well as the similarities between meditation and psychotherapy. Personal qualities that we must cultivate to begin the process of meditation and to sustain an ongoing practice are detailed, including openness, curiosity, effort, persistence, simplicity, tranquility, and mindfulness. The final section discusses the importance of applying the principles and approaches of meditation to daily activity. It is important to have a meditative perspective in everyday life. Besides experiencing the individual joy and calmness that meditation brings into our lives, meditation in action helps us develop compassion and generosity for others. The goal of meditation is to live fully in the world and at the same time not be overly attached to it, and to try to attain higher levels of awareness and then share this knowledge to help others on their journey through life.

Part II is called Meditation and Health. This section explores medical research on the benefits of meditation in such areas as decreasing levels of hormones related to the stress response, controlling high blood pressure, and helping depression, anxiety, and obsessive-compulsive disorder. The mechanism of the stress response is outlined, followed by a detailed description of how meditation and breathing techniques help us better control the autonomic nervous system and other brain functions. While meditation is almost always safe to practice, the last section discusses situations and conditions where a person should not attempt to meditate unless it is part of a more extensive therapeutic process.

Part III is called Meditation Theory and Philosophy. This section deals with the underlying concepts of the philosophical systems Tantra, Samkhya, and Vedanta. These great schools of thought form the theoretical basis and provide the actual techniques for the type of meditation presented in this book. The five components of the mind that are presented are thoughts, the sensory-integration component, the sense of self, decision making, and memory. These aspects of the mind are all strengthened by the practice of meditation. The system of *raja* yoga is described in detail because the form of meditation presented in this book closely follows the eight steps on this path. This includes five restraints on behavior and five observances to prepare us mentally for meditation, the postures and practices of *hatha* yoga, breathing exercises, withdrawal of the senses to deeper states of awareness, concentration techniques, sustained concentration (the actual definition of meditation), and absorption with the highest states of consciousness.

In order to deepen meditation, we must have an object on which to concentrate. These objects, which need to have the inherent ability to guide the practitioner to expanded levels of awareness, are generally *chakras* (energy centers in the body), *mantras* (subtle inner vibrations), *yantras* (geometric shapes that reflect a condensation of the seen and unseen universe), and the breath (control of energy or *prana* within the body). Several sections in this part focus on these powerful objects of concentration. Since the form of meditation presented in this book uses concentration techniques focused on the *chakras*, a detailed, colored image of the *chakras* appears on the front cover of this book. This can be used as a visual guide to the more complex meditation practice presented in Part V.

Part IV is called Preparing for Meditation. This part focuses on the techniques used to prepare the body, breath, and mind for meditation. We analyze the relationship between *hatha* yoga and meditation. *Hatha* yoga postures are useful not only to improve flexibility, but also to strengthen the spine so the practitioner can sit for longer meditations. In the next chapter, there are descriptions of several sitting postures used during meditation. Breathing techniques (*pranayama*) are discussed in detail because these breathing exercises have many important functions in the process of meditation. They have positive effects on the body and mind, helping such health related concerns as sinus problems, hypertension, thyroid disease, and anxiety. *Pranayama* also is very important in helping to focus the mind for deeper meditation, and there are specific techniques that help to activate latent energy in the body (*kundalini*). The following chapter explores the idea of *kundalini*, or latent energy that is stored in the first *chakra*, located in the lowest part of the spine. This primal force is activated and moved upwards to the higher *chakras* during meditation, and as it moves through the seven major *chakras*, physical, psychological, and spiritual transformations occur. As consciousness moves up through the *chakras*, we begin to feel more secure, are able to direct our sexual energy appropriately, develop a stronger sense of self (ego), and become more compassionate, creative, and intuitive.

Part V is called How to Meditate. This part describes the preparations necessary to begin a meditation practice as well as the specific meditation technique itself. Creating a quiet, comfortable environment that is free from distractions is very important in establishing a consistent and deep meditation practice. In the next section, the actual meditation technique is divided into several phases so that readers can systematically and slowly develop their own practice at their own speed. It is designed so that a person can choose to practice simple diaphragmatic breathing and breath awareness to relax and focus his/her thoughts. The reader can also choose the greater complexity of using *mantras* and concentrating on moving energy through the *chakras* with the goal of experiencing more expanded states of consciousness. The final chapter briefly describes meditation techniques that can be practiced by more advanced students who are working closely with an experienced teacher.

The first four parts of this book describe the benefits, practical applications, and underlying theory of meditation. This important background information helps students understand the physical, mental, and spiritual significance of each meditation practice. The fifth and final part is a practical guide that, if systematically followed, can slowly help the individual feel inner calmness, joy, compassion for others, and ultimately to experience expanded states of consciousness.

Part I

What Is Meditation?

1. Definition and Goals

Meditation is sustained and uninterrupted concentration that leads to a highly focused mind. Meditation begins with concentration, which helps make the mind steady. When prolonged concentration leads to the continuous flow of the mind towards one object, this becomes meditation. To maintain and deepen meditation, the mind must have something to focus on. These objects of concentration not only focus the mind but also have the inherent ability to lead the student to more expanded states of awareness. The objects typically used are sounds (*mantras*), visual images (*yantras* or *chakras*), light, breath, or specific types of prayer. Because of their great importance to the form of meditation presented in this book, *chakras*, *mantras*, and *yantras* will be discussed more thoroughly in Part III.

There are several specific goals of meditation. The first is to liberate the mind from disturbing and distracting emotions, thoughts, and desires. The mind is transformed from a state of unrest and disharmony to a state of calmness and equilibrium. Another important goal of meditation is to bring the unconscious mind into conscious awareness in order to gain greater control over thought processes and emotions. The ultimate goal is to attain expanded states of consciousness in which we not only have increased awareness of previously unconscious thoughts and feelings, but also awareness of more subtle and universal principles, and comprehension of the world in a more complex and integrated way. In this state, we can experience great joy and inner peace.

Neutral and nonjudgmental observation of the content and experiences of the mind should accompany the process of meditation. It is important to avoid being attached to the contents of the mind during meditation because the desire to attain something or to have certain types of experiences distracts the mind from its focus and will interfere with continued concentration. This can lead to losing the calmness and contentment that normally characterize the steady mind.

As the power of concentration develops through the practice of meditation, our physical and mental abilities may also increase. It is important not to use these abilities for selfish purposes because this would interfere with the development of compassion and humility, which are very important qualities that arise from deep meditative practices. Self-indulgence and the need for self-gratification limit us to the narrow confines of our own individual mind and inhibit the experience of expanded states of awareness.

The technique of meditation is actually quite simple and systematic. When practicing meditation, we sit on a chair or on the floor with a straight spine and with hands placed comfortably on the lap, thighs, or knees. The eyes are closed gently. Using our mind, we relax each body part, beginning at the head and ending at the feet. We then regulate breathing by using the abdomen and diaphragm to move air in and out of the lungs. During inhalation the upper part of the abdomen moves out, away from the body, and on exhalation the abdomen moves back towards the body. Next, we adjust our breathing rhythm to become efficient, smooth, deep, and without pauses or hesitations. We then withdraw our senses from the outside world and direct all attention inwards. We follow this by concentrating on a sound (*mantra*) and also on specific energy centers within the body (*chakra*s). There is a more detailed explanation of this form of meditation in chapter 24, The Technique of Meditation.

During meditation, when thoughts, emotions, or desires arise, we observe the nature and content of these mental phenomena. We do not force our thinking to stop but instead we allow our thoughts to cease on their own. We simply return our focus to the object of concentration, such as our *mantra*. As thoughts arise, they are allowed to gently come into the mind and then to pass effortlessly out. We calmly bring our focus back to the object of concentration. Slowly, the process of letting go and refocusing becomes easier and is accomplished more quickly and meditation deepens naturally. With persistent practice, the mind gradually becomes identified with the object of concentration. This allows the individual to experience deeper and more highly refined states of consciousness.

Meditation has three key components: the person who is meditating, the technique of meditation, and the object of concentration during meditation. As the practice deepens, awareness of the technique is gradually eliminated. This occurs because as focus on the object of concentration becomes steady and automatic, awareness of the process diminishes until finally we cease to be conscious of it at all. Next, we lose awareness of ourselves as the mind identifies completely with the object of concentration. Finally, the object of concentration itself disappears as the mind becomes completely permeated with the object by its constant association with it. After all three components have disappeared, there is no awareness of our separateness and we experience a state of expanded consciousness.[1]

2. Higher States of Consciousness

The underlying philosophic premise of meditation is that the individual human is both a separate being with an individual consciousness and is also part of a greater universal consciousness. The individual is like a wave, which has a distinct form yet is part of the larger ocean. The body and mind are vehicles through which the universe reveals itself. All energy and matter that exist in the universe also exist in the individual body. By analyzing and exploring the body and mind, we are able to analyze the entire universe. In this context, the purpose of meditation in our lives is to analyze our inner self (microcosm), thereby unfolding the basic reality of the universe (macrocosm). Thus, meditation helps raise individual consciousness to experience and merge with universal consciousness.

In meditation theory, consciousness is the intelligent force and underlying substrate of the entire cosmos from which all energy and matter are created. Merging our mind into this underlying stream of consciousness allows us to gain access to universal energy and experience expanded awareness. Here the sense of self merges with an all-encompassing experience of unity and oneness. We realize we are at one with the entire seen and unseen universe and as a consequence all loneliness, feelings of aloneness, and fear of the unknown disappear. A great sense of freedom, feelings of joy, and waves of beauty and bliss accompany this state of expanded consciousness.

In meditation, our mind is centered and focused for an extended period of time and is not distracted by random thoughts, emotions, or desires. When this happens, our mind can then be directed to move beyond conscious and unconscious thoughts in order to experience expanded and higher levels of consciousness. Experiencing expanded consciousness means that we are open to the world beyond the small sense of self and are willing to enter into the boundless consciousness from which life comes. Awareness can then expand further and further until it encompasses everything and becomes one with the universe.

As our mind perceives these highly refined states in meditation, it is possible to become aware of the ultimate essence of life and existence, the center of pure consciousness. This is the source of the intelligent force that creates, underlies, and pervades the entire universe. Experiencing the center of consciousness has profound effects on the individual. By establishing our awareness in this center of consciousness, we gain access to the manifestations, forces, and mysteries of existence. A more detailed discussion of this subject can be found in chapter 18, *Koshas*: The Five Levels of Consciousness and Holistic Medicine and in chapter 13, *Raja* Yoga: The Integrated Path of Meditation.

According to the philosophy of Vedanta, when meditation leads to a fully conscious and enlightened state, the person realizes that the experience of life and the world of phenomena are really illusion (*maya*). They represent merely a reflection of the reality and truth of higher consciousness. *Maya* does not mean that the world is devoid of all reality, only that it is not what it appears to be. Just as we awaken from sleep to realize that what had seemed real was only a dream, so do we awaken in the highest state of consciousness to realize that our daily life is only seemingly real.

Our life is not simply a hallucination, nor is life arbitrary or meaningless. Identification with our body and mind, however, is similar to seeing the temporary formation of a cloud as permanent. It indeed has form, but it is impermanent and eventually its existence disappears, evaporating back into the air from which it came, just as the mind merges into a more universal awareness in deep meditation. From this perspective, the only reality that is absolute is the all-encompassing, underlying whole. *Maya* involves mistaking parts of the whole for the whole itself.

The idea of *maya* helps explain a great paradox. While the stated goal of meditation -- to attain an enlightened, more comprehensive, and higher state of consciousness -- seems far away and difficult to accomplish, it is actually very close at hand. The philosophy of meditation teaches that human beings are special beings, full of light, born complete and whole, and constantly and intimately connected to all the underlying forces of the universe. People learn to become individuals and separate as they grow, often resulting in the loss of their sense of wholeness. Everyone is already enlightened and complete, but knowledge of this is obscured by the mind, thoughts, desires, and emotions. In this sense, the transformation brought on by meditation is a process of peeling away layers of illusion to awaken to our true selves, encompassing all the power, creative force, and energy of the universe. Thus, striving for enlightenment is itself an illusion (*maya*). We are already there, and it is only the awareness of enlightenment that is obscured.

3. Different Forms of Meditation

Systematic approaches to meditation in the Eastern traditions began in India. The Sanskrit word for meditation is *dhyana*. The practices later spread through Tibet to China and the word became *chan*. The name was further changed in Japan to *zen*.[2] Within the last one hundred years, students in the West have become familiar with these meditative techniques as teachers from Asia have shared their knowledge with prepared and eager students.

The meditation practices presented in this book represent an integrated approach based on the great Indian philosophies of Tantra, Samkhya, and Vedanta. These philosophies also provide the theoretical and practical foundation of *chakras*, *mantras*, and *yantras*, the objects of concentration used in this form of meditation.

Tantra is a philosophy that emphasizes personal experimentation and specific meditative practices. Tantra helps define the subtle energy centers (*chakras*) on which to meditate and the pathways (*nadis*) through which energy is channeled to the highest centers of consciousness. It describes how pure consciousness manifests into individual being.

Samkhya philosophy is the applied and experiential foundation of the eight steps of *raja* yoga. *Raja* is a Sanskrit word meaning "royal" or "king-like" and yoga means to "yoke" or to "unite." Thus, *raja* yoga refers to a powerful and systematic path of uniting individual consciousness with universal consciousness by using specific types of physical exercises (*hatha* yoga postures), breathing techniques (*pranayama*), and concentration and meditation practices. Samkhya also provides the underlying philosophy for *The Yoga Sutras*, a book compiled and codified 1500 to 2000 years ago by the ancient Indian philosopher Patanjali. This short treatise explains yoga and meditation theory and details many spiritual disciplines and practices. *The Yoga Sutras* also describes the powers and experiences that result from attaining the highest states of consciousness.

Vedanta philosophy describes the theoretical foundation of the mind and how it is affected by meditation as well as the mind's relationship to different and expanded states of consciousness. Vedanta is an intellectual system of knowledge based on ancient books called the Upanishads and Vedas. At the heart of this philosophy is the idea that in reality, there is no separation or duality between consciousness, mind, energy, and matter. All that exists is ultimate, unified, and singular consciousness. Separation of body and spirit and all changes in the universe are only illusion. The changeless underlying substructure of pure consciousness is the only truth. This differs in a fundamental way from Samkhya philosophy, which maintains that consciousness and matter coexist simultaneously.

There are several other Eastern-based meditation systems. Tibetan Buddhists have several different techniques of meditation including some brief practices to quickly center the mind and others that are more complex. One interesting technique involves instructing students to listen quietly both to the sounds around them and to the space the sounds create in order to become aware of the void. The void implies having an empty mind, free of distracting thoughts and desires. When the mind is empty, a person can be completely filled with higher forms of knowledge. In Zen Buddhism, meditation often uses counting the breath as a focus of concentration. Chinese Taoists often use slow meditative movements such as tai chi with breath awareness as a form of meditative practice.

Meditation practices exist in all Western religions but they are generally restricted to more serious and advanced students and are not taught to the general public. Most people lack the interest, necessary discipline, or desire for introspection to follow the meditative procedures. Among the major Western religions, however, there are rich traditions of meditation practiced by Jewish students of the Kabbalah, by Christian monks, and by Sufis of the Islamic religion. In these three great religious traditions, meditation itself is often separated from the more formal liturgy because the meditation practices represent experiential disciplines for the development of consciousness. While meditation can enhance a person's understanding of his or her own faith, it can also be practiced separately from religious traditions.

Among the Sufis, twirling movements and ecstatic dance along with recitation of prayers are used as a meditative practice. Christian meditation generally uses prayer as a focus of concentration. In Jewish meditation, one often concentrates on the Hebrew letters that mean God, especially the four letters, *Yod-Heh-Vav-Heh*. Other meditation practices in Judaism include concentrating on the *Shema* prayer, on the *mantra*-like word *Shalom*, and on the tree of life (*sefirot*), which is a concept somewhat similar to the *chakra* system.

4. Misconceptions

Concentration is not meditation, although concentration techniques are used extensively to prepare for deeper meditation. Concentration is focusing the mind on a single object, while meditation is a state that results from sustained and prolonged concentration on a single object.

Meditation does not cause a high, such as one might experience when taking a hallucinogenic drug. While people who explored Eastern forms of meditation in the 1960s and '70s also often experimented with drugs, there are no associations between them. In actuality, mind-altering drugs inhibit a person's ability to concentrate, making deep meditation impossible.

Contemplation is also not meditation. When we say, "I will contemplate and meditate on that idea," we are stating an intention to reflect on a concept with some intensity. But without practicing the systematic regulation of the body and breath, the focus of the mind, and the constant, nonjudgmental awareness of consciousness, this is not meditation.

Meditation does not allow the mind to drift aimlessly. The process of meditation continuously brings the mind back to a single point of concentration and discourages reverie, daydreaming, and wandering of the mind.

The goal of meditation is not to achieve altered states, to see colors, or to have unusual auditory or visual experiences. While extrasensory experiences may occur, we are encouraged to practice nonattachment, to simply observe these inner phenomena, and to let the images go. After observing with dispassion, we gently return to the focus of concentration.

Meditation is not religious, although religion and a belief in a higher force can enhance the meditative process. Meditation can enhance our understanding of religion. All the great religious traditions practice a form of meditation though this may not be commonly known or frequently taught.

Meditation is not prayer, although certain prayers can be used as a focus of concentration. Prayers are tools to change our attitudes or to inspire us to appreciate higher spiritual ideals. True prayer is not an appeal to receive something or to become happier. Deep prayer focuses on self-surrender and offering oneself to others or to a higher principle, such as God. Prayer helps a person be less self-interested and self-centered. Prayer can lead to increased humility and feelings of forgiveness. All these attributes and experiences of prayer can help the meditative process.[3]

5. The Benefits

While practicing meditation we learn to slow the rapid movements of thoughts across the conscious mind. Meditation then trains our mind to become more focused, proficient, and creative and less scattered, chaotic, and disorganized. Through meditation, we learn to use our will and the decision-making component of our mind to direct our thoughts. (For a more detailed description of the five components of the mind, refer to chapter 12, The Mind.) We learn to think in different ways, gaining newer and richer inner mental experiences. The mind becomes more like the concentrated and powerful light coming from a laser beam and less like the weak light emanating from a light bulb.

Meditation enhances our awareness of how our body, breath, senses, conscious mind, and unconscious mind interact. This expanded awareness helps us see clearly, discriminate wisely, and make good decisions about our physical and emotional health. A physician who practices holistic medicine may use meditative techniques as part of his/her therapy to treat various medical and emotional concerns and illnesses.

During meditation feelings and thoughts that were previously hidden and unconscious rise into conscious awareness. Generally, unpleasant feelings and thoughts do not simply go away if they are avoided. Instead they get buried in the subconscious or unconscious like dust buried under a rug. When this occurs, we rarely have control over these thoughts, yet the train of associations arising from them affects our behavior. Meditation can act in ways similar to psychotherapy because it allows for these unconscious thoughts and emotions to rise to the surface. Here they are observed and impartially scrutinized and we can make a decision whether to take action on our concerns or to simply let them go. We learn to think what we want to think, when we want to think it, and how we want to think it. We learn to be in control of the moment and in stressful situations resist the emotional and psychological pressures from the unconscious. As practitioners of meditation we learn to be in control, directing our will to do what we want to do and to not do what we do not want to do. Advanced teachers of meditation describe this ability as self-mastery.

The Benefits of Meditation
Slows the thinking process
Enhances awareness of body and mind
Brings to conscious awareness feelings that are unconscious
Helps us experience each moment more fully
Helps us observe our feelings without judgment
Helps us stay in the present
Releases unpleasant memories and anxiety
Eliminates dependency on other people and objects
Helps us become aware of shared experiences with others
Increases compassion for others
Helps us practice loving kindness and generosity
Teaches us to accept ourselves
Explores the four levels of consciousness
Helps us experience higher states of consciousness

When we meditate regularly we experience each moment with heightened awareness and greater clarity. For example, when viewing a beautiful sunset, we might be somewhat distracted by thoughts of work, feeling hungry, or worries of being late for some future obligation. Our attention does not stay completely focused on the sunset scene. As a consequence, we might not experience the smells in the air, the sounds of birds singing, or the intensity of the colors of the sky. Thus, we would not be fully present. Alternately, as students of meditation we use learned skills of concentration to turn off mental interference and concentrate totally on the whole sensory experience. At the end of meditation, we may notice that colors become more vivid and sounds more melodious. There are no more extraneous images placed between the experience of the sunset and us. In a sense, we become one with the total experience. As a result, we become more aware of subtle phenomena that are otherwise not apparent to us, and our world becomes deeper and richer.

During meditation we watch feelings arise with a quiet, nonjudging awareness. This allows us to carefully observe the contents of our mind. We also learn to trace our emotions to their source. Meditation helps us let go of distracting emotions that bind us. We learn to experience the totality of feelings, yet not be enslaved by them. By following the path of meditation, we learn to feel the wide range of human feelings in an intense and direct way, including the unpleasant emotions of anger, jealousy, fear, and sadness. At the same time, meditation teaches us not to overly indulge these feelings and to avoid hanging on to or surrendering to them. Ultimately, meditation leads to liberation from disturbing and distracting emotions, thoughts, and desires, and replaces these disturbances with a sense of inner quiet, freedom, and joy.

In meditation we learn to stay in the present, to let go of troublesome memories, and to release anxiety of the future. Meditation is not about acquiring new experiences or getting to any different place, but rather involves accepting what we already have and being where we already are. We learn to be here now. Meditation then helps expand the moment--we experience the fullness of the moment and realize its full potentiality. In the philosophy of Zen Buddhism, this is called beginner's mind. As we practice meditation, we become willing to begin each moment as a new and life-enhancing experience. Each time we sit for meditation, the experience is fresh and alive.[4]

When we meditate we do not withdraw from the world but from dependence on objects and people as sources of gratification. The process of meditation teaches us that we often seek happiness through desiring external objects. Turbulence of the mind is based upon the type of desire we have, especially when we want more than what is necessary for healthy and comfortable living. When a desire arises, we often become dissatisfied because we find ourselves separated from the source of satisfaction. We suffer because we are worried we will not attain what we want or are afraid we will lose what we already have. Through meditation we realize that the true source of happiness does not reside in attained objects and goals but in a state of mind that is independent of these objects. When we practice meditation we realize that we are truly content when we are free from desires.[5]

In meditation we begin to understand that all human beings are part of the same underlying universal consciousness, just as all drops of water in the ocean share all the qualities of the ocean. Meditation helps relationships because the student realizes that all people share similar types of feelings, experiences, and qualities. We begin to see the reflection of ourselves in others and begin to relate to others as we relate to ourselves. Other people are seen not as objects to get something from but as fellow travelers on the same path of life.

This experience of inner relatedness results in our being able to feel compassion and empathy for others. We learn to practice loving kindness, express generosity, and have gentle speech in our relationships. As meditation progresses, we learn to let go of the pain and sorrows of past losses and betrayals. The heart releases its disappointments and expands and we learn to direct loving kindness even to people we may dislike or who have hurt or threatened us. Patience, tolerance, and forgiveness are mature qualities that develop as a result of practicing loving kindness.

We learn to accept ourselves when we practice meditation regularly. As we sit quietly in meditation, we become aware of unpleasant emotions, physical pain, or fears of death, disease, poverty, or injustice. During the process of meditation, we learn to have an accepting attitude towards each of these negative feelings and experiences. Because we develop a tolerant attitude towards our own fears and unease, and at the same time realize that all humans have similar anxieties and apprehensions, we learn to feel compassion for other people's suffering as well. Seen in this light, compassion is an intense and sincere feeling that rises spontaneously in our own heart to help relieve the pain of others.

Meditation helps us explore the four levels of consciousness, which are waking, dreaming, deep sleep, and sleepless sleep (*turiya*). This last level is a highly conscious state similar to deep sleep except we remain totally awake and aware. Every human has potential access to this highly aware and peaceful state of consciousness because it is constantly and permanently available to experience, but most individuals are too distracted and preoccupied by their thoughts and desires. Meditation can provide the necessary techniques to consciously experience sleepless sleep.

While the ultimate goal of meditation is not to experience altered states of consciousness, there are some experiences that result from meditation that are quite interesting and life trans-forming. Some people develop panscopic vision, which involves the ability to perceive an object from all sides at once. There are descriptions of being able to visualize with the mind's eye more than the three dimensions that our physical eyes normally see. Barriers between the senses are lowered and people sometimes describe being able to see sounds and fragrances or to hear colors. Extrasensory perception including clairvoyance and telepathy, can also be an outcome of intense concentration practices.[6] Advanced teachers of meditation always warn their students to view these phenomena with simple curiosity, with neutrality and dispassion, and never to use these abilities to impress, manipulate, or harm another person.

The benefits of meditation can be understood by the following analogy. The human mind is like the ocean, the conscious mind representing the surface of the sea and the innumerable fluctuations of thought and emotion representing the ocean waves. Lying beneath the surface is the unconscious mind, analogous to the deep and submerged ocean expanse. The turbulence of the thought waves obscures the depths of knowledge underneath the conscious mind in a similar way that ocean waves make it impossible to see beneath the ocean surface. The process of meditation calms the tumultuous ebb and flow of the mind's outer layer of wave activity like a calm day quiets the ocean surface. Unconscious repression and habits deep within the mind are allowed to rise to the surface to be observed, in a similar way that bubbles and currents rise and dissipate on the ocean surface. Since no energy is supplied to suppress them, the bubbles gently burst and dissipate. This dispassion averts the creation in the unconscious of further increased psychological pressure that can produce exaggerated emotional reactions, like tidal waves in the ocean. The conscious mind becomes quiet and still, and the deeper mysterious layers of the unconscious can be observed and experienced, similar to the way the ocean depths become visible on a calm, wind-free day. Finally, the individual, separate self merges with universal consciousness, like a wave that merges with the great ocean expanse. True knowledge and tranquility result and the individual experiences the peace and bliss of universal consciousness.[7]

6. Qualities Necessary to Practice Meditation

While it may seem that sitting quietly and concentrating on an object is a simple thing to do, the practice of meditation can be difficult and demanding. This is the great paradox of meditation. There are several important qualities that we must cultivate to begin the process of meditation, to sustain an ongoing practice, and to consistently progress on our spiritual path towards true compassion for others and expanded consciousness. While these qualities need to be present to some extent before initiating a meditation practice, consistent practice of meditation will also cultivate, nurture, and enhance these qualities.[8]

When embarking on the path of meditation, we need to be open to seeing things from a larger perspective. Openness means that we are willing to expand our outlook from being narrow and self-involved to a more global and encompassing orientation. Being open also means we allow ourselves to be vulnerable, to admit weakness, and to acknowledge our own insecurities.

In order to maintain an ongoing meditation practice, we generally have an inherent curiosity and desire to learn more about ourselves, our relationships with other human beings, and with the universe around us. There is a curiosity to know the inner essence of things. The questions "who am I?" and "where did I come from?" are of paramount importance. There is a desire to investigate the underlying mysteries of life.

Because human beings are always distracted by the pleasures, attachments, and habits associated with life, a great amount of effort and energy need to be generated to maintain a consistent meditation practice. It takes effort and discipline to foster healthy living habits and avoid getting entangled in unwholesome lifestyles.

Being persistent is important to our meditative practice because each time the mind wanders in meditation, we must gently bring it back to the object of concentration. Each time the mind drifts off and is then gently brought back to focus on the object of concentration, the mind gets retrained and this creates new positive habits for the thinking process. Positive images, inspirational ideas, and spiritual notions often replace negative thinking patterns. Progress is always being made when we meditate regularly as this underlying transformation process occurs unconsciously and continuously.

Qualities Necessary to Practice Meditation
Openness
Curiosity
Effort
Persistence
Simplicity
Courage
Patience
Tranquility
Calmness
Joy
Mindfulness

We need to practice simplicity of thought, deed, and action to help create an environment conducive for meditation. Desiring more luxuries and external comforts than is necessary to satisfy our basic needs can create complexities in life that interfere with attaining a concentrated mind. On the physical level, eating simple foods low in saturated fat, salt, and sugar allows for better health and greater clarity of thought. Getting enough exercise and sleep as well as directing our sexual energy appropriately free the mind to go inwards. Practicing simplicity on the mental and emotional levels means avoiding useless gossip, reading meaningless or offensive literature, or thinking irrelevant or disturbing thoughts, all of which dissipate our energy. Balance and moderation are essential for creating a meditative inner environment.

The quality of courage is necessary to help maintain a spiritual and meditative practice and lifestyle. There are innumerable obstacles on the path to enlightenment and doubts are commonplace. When practicing meditation we may ask ourselves, "Why am I sitting here watching my thoughts, practicing being aware of my breathing patterns, and repeating a mental sound?" Because meditation involves self-scrutiny and self-observation, we may experience uncomfortable moments of anger, greed, jealousy, fear, or sadness. It takes courage to free our hearts and minds from these emotions.

Patience is vital on the path of meditation. There are moments when a person feels like nothing is happening in spite of regular or intense meditative practices. Discouragement is quite common and progress is often slow. The desire for sensory or sexual pleasures, laziness, boredom, restlessness, and feelings of doubt all can disturb and disrupt the process of meditation. These distracting experiences are to be expected. We need to learn to be patient and confident that through consistent practice these hindrances will be overcome in time. The journey on the path of enlightenment is ongoing and we must be persistent, sincere, and diligent. It is often said that breakthroughs to higher perception levels occur when we finally let go of the need for results.

Tranquility involves the capacity of the mind to be calm in the busy, modern world. In meditation we need to allow the body, breath, and mind to settle down, to remain silent and alert. The process of meditation will further foster stillness and a sense of peacefulness. Tranquility ensues when we give up the futile effort to control everything and instead greet each moment with openness and calmness.

While a certain degree of calmness and equanimity are necessary to effectively practice meditation, we can also gradually strengthen these qualities by practicing meditation consistently. Calmness and equanimity are reflections of our ability to remain centered and unaffected by changing circumstances. Life's many vicissitudes and demands constantly challenge us. Equanimity involves strength of will and flexibility of body and mind to respond carefully, quickly, and effortlessly to life's problems. It involves being passive at times when avoidance is called for and to react actively when more vigorous responses are necessary.

The quality of joy arising during meditation and providing inspiration for continued practice is unlike the temporary pleasurable feelings that come from having a desire satisfied. Joy arising from meditation is different from the experience of simple pleasure because it arises from feelings of the unification of our own body, heart, mind, and consciousness with universal forces greater than ourselves. The effects of this type of joy have been described as feelings of bliss or rapture. Joy that is cultivated by a meditative practice also involves living life with a lightness of heart, a sense of humor, and gentleness of action, speech, and spirit. By learning not to take life and its innumerable experiences too seriously, each moment is enjoyed more fully, while at the same time there is an awareness of the ever-changing and ephemeral nature of life.

Cultivating mindfulness helps us deepen our meditation practice. Being mindful means having clear awareness of what is happening at all times and at each moment. It is the ability to see how things really are. It also involves listening carefully to what is being said. Mindfulness means to be fully present and to practice conscious living at all times with respect to the body, senses, mind, and emotions. If a person consistently drifts or is distracted during meditation and does not practice mindfulness, meditation will be less effective and more difficult.

7. Application to Daily Living: Meditation in Action

It is very important to have a meditative perspective during everyday life. By learning to apply the principles and approaches of meditation to daily activity, the entire day can be transformed into a meditative experience. In order to have real practical value, meditation should also provide direction and inspiration to our daily life as well as help to cultivate a sense of calmness, peace, and joy throughout the waking hours. Meditation is not simply sitting quietly for twenty to sixty minutes once a day, but is also a process of learning to be poised, strong, and focused amidst the dramas and vicissitudes of life.

Meditation in action involves being in the present, being an objective observer and a careful listener. It involves being constantly mindful, which means paying attention and being fully present in the moment, no matter what the activity. In sitting meditation, we learn to focus the mind, and in meditation in action we apply this learned ability to concentrate on the various activities and responsibilities of life. Whether the actions or circumstances are enjoyable or unpleasant, we try to experience them with a calm attitude.

Application to Daily Living: Meditation in Action
Be in the present
Appreciate the fullness of the now
Let go of negative habits
See the value in all situations
Do not be attached to objects of the world
Enjoy the world with a sense of humor
Improve communication
Practice loving kindness and compassion
Self study and introspection
Practice mindfulness in activities and relationships
Focus on the breath and mantra

Because meditation in action involves always returning to the moment, we learn to appreciate the fullness of the now. This can be accomplished by momentarily reflecting on life's most simple activities such as: pausing to think about the wonders of language before reading the newspaper; taking a full breath for an instant and appreciating how fortunate it is that there is money in the bank before writing a check; smiling broadly that we have a car to drive when stuck in a traffic jam; giving thanks for the availability of food before eating; or stopping for a moment to appreciate life and our health when sending love to a sick friend.

Meditation as applied to daily living teaches us to let go of negative habits and addictions. During meditation we learn to calm our restless mind and to let go of preoccupations. This allows us to see clearly without the distortions of fear and worry. By practicing this attitude during everyday life, we learn how to navigate through difficult times with a sense of clarity and purpose. This improves the ability to quickly assess a situation by seeing the whole picture more clearly and leads to making appropriate and intelligent decisions.

Meditation in action involves seeing value in all situations and learning to find meaning in both positive and negative experiences in life. We learn that even illness, loss, or pain can create opportunities for growth. Life becomes a learning process and we look at what life gives us as an opportunity to grow. We take responsibility for our actions in all situations and accept the consequences when we make mistakes.

We learn how to use and enjoy the luxuries and objects of the world, but at the same time we do not get attached to them. By practicing meditation in action we realize that our happiness is independent of our house, car, and other material possessions. We are deeply immersed in life, yet remain free from the need to accumulate more than what is necessary for healthy living. We learn to enjoy the complexities of daily life but are able to avoid getting bound by its many entanglements.

Meditation in action involves enjoying the world with a sense of lightness and humor. We learn to see clearly the impermanence and changeability of life and realize how pointless it is to take ourselves too seriously.

Because meditation leads to a more concentrated mind, we learn to think more clearly and to act and react in the world with greater skill and more precision. The ability to communicate becomes more honest and direct, often resulting in improved and more trusting interpersonal relationships.

As we commit to the meditative path, we practice loving kindness and compassion and become devoted and truthful with our family and community. Because we see that all people share our same concerns and needs, we see ourselves reflected in the minds and hearts of others. We learn to treat others with respect, humility, and generosity of the heart.

Meditation in action can also involve self-study and introspection, such as reading books and poetry written by inspiring people and keeping a diary or journal. We can also visualize the coming day upon awakening in the morning, or practice retrospection before going to sleep by recollecting the events of the day from latest to earliest.

There are several ways to practice meditation in action. One way is to simply practice mindfulness in both daily activities and in relationships. As we do when we practice sitting meditation, we try to stay focused, aware, alert, and open at all times. We bring the clarity, calmness, and joy that are experienced in meditation into our active lives.

Another way to practice meditation in action is to stay focused on our *mantra* or breath. This can be done any time throughout the day and can be especially useful when in stressful situations or during periods of anxiety. Breath awareness or mentally repeating the *mantra* can also be practiced while walking, exercising, driving a car, or eating. This will help keep our mind centered so we can fully enjoy the present, make appropriate decisions, and remain calm when facing the many challenges of life.

Part II

Meditation and Health

8. Medical Research on Health Benefits

Most of the medical research into the health benefits of meditation has focused on one of the following forms of meditation. Meditation based on Zen philosophy uses breath awareness as its object of concentration. Transcendental Meditation (TM), a system practiced by followers of Maharishi Mahesh Yogi, uses specific *mantras* as its focus. Clinically Standardized Meditation is an unstructured western-derived practice that uses various non-*mantra* sounds without breath awareness as a focus of concentration. Herbert Benson, a physician who has done research on the relaxation response, developed a meditative system called Respiratory One Method. This form of meditation uses repetition of the word "one" coordinated with the breath. Mindfulness Meditation (*Vipassana*) is a Buddhist derived system that encourages observation of thoughts and images with a nonjudgmental attitude and has no specific object of concentration. *Kundalini* Yogic Meditation uses breathing techniques and *mantra* as a focus of concentration.

The Tantra/Samkhya/Vedanta form of meditation based on the eight principles of *raja* yoga that is described in this book uses an integrated method of breath, *mantras*, *yantras*, and *chakra*s as its objects of concentration. It is a system practiced in the Himalayan Mountains of India, Nepal, and Tibet and its tenets and techniques have been handed down from teacher to student for thousands of years. There are many documented health benefits associated with this form of meditation. The ultimate goal of this meditative tradition goes beyond its positive health effects and involves the desire to experience more expanded states of awareness. These more comprehensive states are often difficult to quantify because they tend to be non-verbal, experiential, and anecdotal.

The following information on the various physiologic and psychological benefits of the above-mentioned forms of meditation is primarily based on two excellent books that summarize many research studies in clear and comprehensive ways. These books are *Zen and the Brain* by J. Austin and *Complementary & Alternative Medicine* by L. Freeman and G. F. Lawlis.[9]

On a physical level, meditation slows the release of hormones in response to stress, including cortisol from the adrenal glands and thyroid stimulating hormone (TSH) and growth hormone (GH) from the pituitary gland in the brain. There are increased levels of the hormone DHEA-S that comes from the adrenals, which are generally lower as people age. There is decreased amount of corticotrophin-releasing hormone (CRH) secreted from the hypothalamus in the brain, which has the effect of slowing the physiological responses to stressful events.

Other important physiologic changes that result from meditation are a decline in the blood lactate level, which indicates the body is reacting less to stressful situations. Oxygen consumption is lowered to a level generally only seen after many hours of sleep. There is less suppression of immunity in response to stressful events. There are lower amounts of the CD8+ cells, which are inhibitors of the important immune enhancing T cells.

Practicing meditation has been of benefit in treating many diseases. People with heart disease have fewer palpitations and abnormal rhythms, including premature ventricular contractions and supraventricular contractions. In general, heart and respiratory rates decrease. Chronic medical conditions have been helped, such as hypertension, chronic pain, insomnia, chronic fatigue syndrome, irritable bowel syndrome, menopausal symptoms, hot flashes, and seizures.

Meditation has important benefits on the emotional and psychological levels. Depression can be helped because meditation increases serotonin availability and increases tryptophan in the central nervous system, both of which are important for mood elevation. Substance abuse problems, such as alcoholism, cigarette smoking, and drug abuse have also been helped by meditation.

Attention to the rhythms of *mantra* recitation and breathing patterns creates an anti-anxiety and calming effect and in a sense acts as a natural tranquilizer. The act of observing and letting go of disturbing thoughts and feelings has a desensitization effect, similar to behavioral therapy. This helps us become less reactive to hidden fears and anxiety and thus can be helpful for generalized panic disorder. Consistent practice results in an increase in feelings of self-confidence, optimism, fewer guilt feelings, and a decrease in unreasonable internal expectations. Improved self-esteem, less intense grief reactions, and diminished separation anxiety are also mentioned as benefits of meditation.

The yoga breathing technique of alternate nostril breathing, described in chapter 21, *Pranayama* and the Breath, can be modified so that both inhalation and exhalation are practiced through the left nostril. This technique has been shown to be effective in obsessive-compulsive disorder. The explanation for this result is that this disorder seems to be associated with less activity in the right side of the brain. By stimulating the left nerve endings in the nose that then cross over to the right side of the brain, there is increased stimulation on the right side of the brain, resulting in the blocking of obsessive and compulsive urges.

There is a shift to a greater balancing of activity between the two hemispheres of the brain during meditation. Generally the left hemisphere is dominant in most people and this side of the brain tends to be responsible for linear, time oriented, and verbal thought. The right brain is more involved with creative, intuitive, and abstract thinking. Since meditation and breathing exercises create more of a balanced effect, there is greater integration between reasoning abilities and creativity. Practicing visualization-based meditative techniques also leads to more creative use of the imagination.

Repetition of the *mantra* or focusing the mind on a continual image causes a blanking out of all thought and decreases responses to internal and external stimulation. The result is a renewed enthusiasm for new stimuli and thought patterns, in a way reminiscent of a young child's excitement to new ideas and experiences. This is similar to the concept of "beginner's mind" described in the Zen Buddhist meditative tradition.

EEG brain patterns often show several types of changes that reflect less anxiety and a more calm mental and emotional state. There are reports of lower amplitudes of all brain wave patterns, reflecting less intense responses to stressful stimuli. Beta activity is reduced, indicating less activation of the frontal brain region, which is the area responsible for emotional reactivity. There are more frontal alpha waves upon exposure to loud noise, which is associated with less anxiety. This alpha activity is not easily blocked even by the sensory stimuli of heat, cold, sound, light, or vibration.

The Menninger Foundation's research with Swami Rama in the early 1970s found that he was able to produce delta brain wave patterns on EEG while remaining totally conscious and aware. This is highly significant because delta waves are found only in deep sleep, the most restful of all human states, in which there are no dreams or rapid eye movements. Remaining wakeful during this relaxed state results in extremely pleasurable and calm experiences. In meditation philosophy, this sleepless sleep (*turiya*) is considered an evolved and expanded state of consciousness.

9. Effects on the Stress Response

The practice of meditation can be of great therapeutic benefit when dealing with stress. Stress can be a disrupting influence affecting physical, emotional, and mental well-being. Symptoms that can occur as a result of stress are anxiety, nervousness, rapid heart-beat, cold and clammy hands, and muscle tension. External events such as bright lights, loud noises, or environmental pollution as well as internal concerns such as fearful thoughts, troublesome memories, or emotional traumas can cause stress. By its effects on the autonomic (involuntary) nervous system and on the endocrine glands, stress literally affects every cell in the body. A wide variety of diseases are attributed to the influence of stress, including hypertension, ulcers, migraine headaches, arthritis, heart disease, and cancer.

In actuality, it is not the stressful event that causes problems, but our response to stress that leads to illness or unhappiness. The stress response itself is a vital and necessary adaptation for survival because it is one of the body's inherent mechanisms for protection. Pulling our hands away from a fire, generating enough strength to beat off an attacker, or activating the immune system to increase the number of white blood cells to kill off invading virulent bacteria are all examples of healthy stress reactions. In normal circumstances, confrontation with a stressor (the agent or factor causing stress) is a self-limited experience because there is a finite period of time when we are being attacked. Generally the stress response has three stages: alarm (or recognition), resistance (or dealing with the stressor), and exhaustion (or recovery, when the organism rests to recuperate from the trauma of the stress). This mechanism works well in sudden and self-limited situations.

Problems occur with the normal stress reaction when the stressors are chronic, as is often the case in crowded urban living conditions where there is constant noise, congestion, and pollution.

The chronic stress response also occurs when a person is plagued by ongoing fear or anxiety. In this situation, the third phase of normal stress response cannot be completed. Without the time for rest and recovery from the exertion of stress, we become exhausted and overwhelmed by a habituated stress response. As a result we feel run-down and weak, with lowered stamina, and eventually resistance is lowered to a point where we become vulnerable to serious disease. The problem, then, is not the stress itself but the prolonged or chronic stress response.

Individuals vary greatly in determining whether or not a situation is stressful. For some, a traffic jam, preparing for a party, or concerns about the welfare of our children are major sources of stress, while for others these situations are not stressful at all. Our psychological and emotional state of mind is crucial in determining how severe a disruptive challenge has to be before it is experienced as stressful.

Meditation can help us learn to develop resilience, inner strength, balance, and adaptability so that the stress threshold is raised. This implies that the stress response is controllable and can be moderated when we are faced with challenges. The goal of meditation is to learn how to observe our thoughts and feelings with an objective awareness and to create a calm inner center. By applying what we experience in the meditative state to life's everyday events, we learn to prevent the stress response from becoming chronic, habitual, or exaggerated.

Breathing techniques, such as diaphragmatic breathing, alternate nostril breathing, and *bhramari* (bee breath) can also be of great benefit to diminish the stress response. These techniques are described in greater detail in chapter 21, *Pranayama and the Breath*. To understand how these exercises help, it is important to understand the physiology of the stress response. This is complex and involves interactions between the central nervous system (brain and spinal cord), autonomic (involuntary) nervous system, endocrine glands (hormones), and the organs, tissues, and cells of the body.[10]

10. The Brain and the Nervous System

We experience a stressful event through one of the five senses (smell, taste, sight, touch, or hearing) or from a thought or feeling. Signals from the organ that receives the stimuli travel via nerves or nerve cells to the brain. The cerebral cortex interprets the event and sends messages to various parts of the body to respond to the stressful occurrence. If signals go to the frontal lobe or the limbic system in the brain, emotions will be experienced. The cerebellum response to activation would be to affect balance and movement. If the hypothalamus or pituitary gland is stimulated, hormones are secreted, which travel to different glands of the body. The endocrine glands (adrenal, thyroid, parathyroid, and sex glands) respond by releasing various hormones, which in turn affect the metabolism and immune system of the body. Another system that is often stimulated by the pituitary gland is the autonomic nervous system.

The autonomic nervous system regulates the involuntary physiologic functions of various internal organ systems such as respiration, pulse rate, blood pressure, reproductive functioning, and digestion. The word "autonomic" implies that these systems work automatically, without the need for conscious volition to direct their functioning. This is in contrast to the muscular-skeletal, or voluntary, nervous system, which regulates voluntary muscle movement. The autonomic nervous system is subdivided into the sympathetic and parasympathetic systems. While these subsystems often work in opposition to each other, the net result of their interaction is to create harmonious regulation (homeostasis). If one of the systems is chronically over-stimulated or under-stimulated, physical illness or emotional problems related to the stress response may occur.

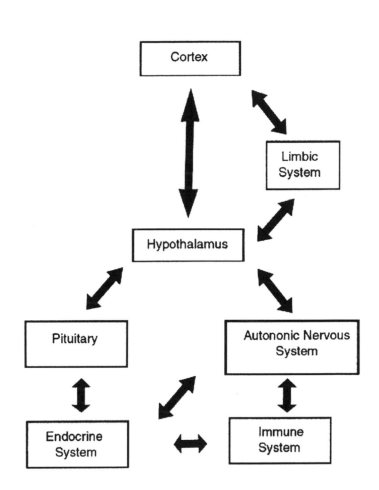

Relationship Between the Brain, Nervous System, Immune System, and the Glands

The sympathetic system controls the active internal processes and is the predominate system in dangerous situations. Activation of the sympathetic nervous system induces the following reactions: pupil dilation, increased blood flow to the heart and brain, and constriction of blood vessels that supply digestion, kidney function, and small muscles. This response is called the fight-or-flight mechanism. When dealing with an emergency, it makes sense for the following things to occur: pupils dilate so a person can see better, the heart speeds up to increase circulation, and the blood vessels constrict so that a larger flow of blood may be directed away from less vital structures to the larger muscles and to the brain to allow for more active responses and clearer thinking. Other changes that occur during activation of the sympathetic nervous system include: tensing of the muscles in the hands, feet, shoulders, and neck; tightening of the throat; and changes in breathing from diaphragmatic to chest breathing or the holding of one's breath.

There are also important interconnections between the sympathetic nervous system and immunity. It is known that sympathetic nerve fibers have contact with and stimulate lymph glands, the spleen, and the thymus gland. These tissues are responsible for producing certain bio-chemicals (cytokines) and lymphocytes (natural killer cells) that regulate the body's ability to fight infection. Increased sympathetic activity causes a marked reduction in the function of these natural killer cells, resulting in increased susceptibility to infectious diseases. The cytokines also communicate with other endocrine glands as well as with brain cells of the hypothalamus, thereby affecting the function of these organs. All these interactions illustrate how stress can affect our body's ability to maintain hormonal balance and to fight off infection.

All these sympathetic nervous system responses are primitive instinctual reactions to danger and serve us well in an emergency. But if these reactions occur on a regular basis in the absence of a real threat, then we will experience the symptoms that characterize the stress response, such as heart pounding, sweaty hands, mind racing, and general muscle tension.

Organ	Sympathetic Nervous System Action	Parasympathetic Nervous System Action
Salivary gland	Stop secretion	Secrete
Heart	Accelerate	Decelerate
Bronchial tubes	Dilate	Constrict
Stomach	Stop secretion of acid	Secrete acid
Intestines	Decreases activity	Increases activity
Bladder	Relax	Contract
Blood vessels	Constrict	Dilate
Pupils of eyes	Dilate	Constrict
Skin temperature	Cooler	Warmer
Muscles	Tense	Relax

The sympathetic nervous system is responsible for stimulating the glands that secrete adrenaline (also called epinephrine), which is the active hormone that causes the afore-mentioned responses. Two large sympathetic nerves running along each side of the spine often stimulate the adrenal glands to secrete adrenaline. It seems reasonable that part of the control afforded by meditation, breathing exercises, and yoga postures in general may be due to the pacification of the sympathetic nervous system. There are several techniques that regulate and pacify this system. During meditation the mind remains calm and emotions are brought under more conscious control, which has the effect of decreasing the release of adrenaline from the nerve endings and glands. Breathing exercises and meditation encourage a strong upright posture that takes the pressure off the nerves that run alongside the spine. By efficient diaphragmatic breathing during meditation, the smooth and efficient movement of the abdominal and back muscles puts less pressure on the adrenal glands, located in the area of the solar plexus, so that it produces a more regulated release of adrenaline.

The other way to balance the sympathetic reactions is to gently stimulate the parasympathetic nervous system. This system is responsible for opposing the reactions initiated by the sympathetic system and is generally associated with relaxation and feelings of well-being. The heart slows, the skin feels mildly flushed because the blood vessels relax, and the mind becomes calm as blood is no longer being hurriedly shunted to the brain. The kidneys and digestive organs become active and the muscles relax.

The main nerves associated with the parasympathetic nervous system are the paired cranial nerves called the vagus nerves. These wandering nerves leave the right and left sides of the brain, cross over to the other side of the body, and have connections to many organs and tissues of the body. Meditation techniques that bring about a calm inner state allow the individual to gain greater control of the activity of the vagus nerves. When the vagus nerves are gently activated, this inhibits secretion of hormones associated with the sympathetic nervous system, resulting in a state of relaxation.

Parasympathetic nerve endings that emanate from and travel to the vagus nerves are also found in the nose, throat, stretch receptors in the lungs, and the chemoreceptors of the carotid artery (carotid bulb). Because these nerves are so closely associated with the organs of respiration and breathing, certain breathing techniques directly stimulate the parasympathetic system. Parasympathetic nerve endings are also found in the nerve plexuses located in major centers in the body, which corresponds to the subtle *chakra*s. Advanced practitioners of meditation who are versed in anatomy and physiology believe that it is control and systematic stimulation of the parasympathetic nervous system, primarily through the right vagus nerve and its nerve endings, that are essential and actively promoted through advanced breathing exercises. Activation of this system through these breathing exercises and through certain concentration techniques is generally associated with relaxation, the slowing of physiological processes, and deeper meditative states.

Alternate nostril breathing is a particular breathing technique that is said to stimulate the right vagus nerve endings in the nose and lungs, which has the effect of enhancing voluntary control of the parasympathetic nervous system. Diaphragmatic breathing practiced along with methods of concentration on the solar plexus area (third *chakra*) also help bring about voluntary control of the parasympathetic nervous system.

After mastering the above-mentioned techniques to consciously stimulate and control parasympathetic nervous system activity, it is then possible to gain greater voluntary control of the hypothalamus located deep within the mid-brain. It is in the hypothalamus where the parasympathetic nervous system sends many of its signals and nerve impulses. From the central controlling center of the hypothalamus, control of the other interconnecting organs and body systems may be gained. This includes the limbic system (emotional center), cerebral cortex (thought and intellectual center), pituitary gland (endocrine gland activity), rhinencephalon (instincts), appetite center, and body temperature center. These close connections may explain how breathing exercises and other meditative techniques allow us, when we are more advanced in meditation, to control our body, mind, and senses.

As in all of life, balance is of utmost importance when dealing with the autonomic nervous system responses. When the sympathetic system is overly or chronically activated, we feel the symptoms of stress leading to illness. If the parasympathetic system is overly activated, we may not react quickly enough to situations that require immediate responses. We may become inappropriately relaxed to the point of being inactive or lazy. The path of meditation, as a complete system, enables us to balance and have greater control over the autonomic nervous system to create physical and mental harmony.[11]

How Breathing Affects Voluntary, Involuntary And Emotional Processes.

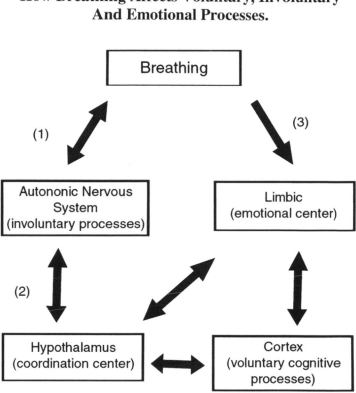

(1) through vagus-parasympathetic nerves (nose receptors, lung stretch receptors, cardiac-celiac plexus, carotid sinuses)
(2) nose (olfactory nerve to rhinencephalon)
(3) parasympathetic nerve

11. When Close Supervision Is Suggested

Meditation is almost always safe and effective as a means to attain spiritual growth or as a treatment for those medical and psychological ailments for which it is indicated. There are a few situations and conditions, however, where a person might not attempt meditating unless it is part of a more extensive therapeutic process. The advice of a skilled meditation teacher who has expertise in the field of psychology should be sought to answer specific questions and to lead the person to appropriate techniques and practices.

People with the psychiatric illness of schizophrenia or who have had psychotic episodes in which they have experienced paranoid feelings should only practice meditation under close supervision of a meditation teacher and mental health care worker. Medication for these serious mental health disorders is almost always necessary. In some cases there can be an exacerbation of depersonalization and preoccupation when meditation is practiced, especially for longer periods of time. When prescribed for these conditions, meditation and simple breathing exercises are practiced for very short periods of time.

People who are excessively narcissistic might experience an intensification of their self-involvement if they practice meditation for long periods. These individuals will need concomitant psychotherapy or close guidance from a meditation teacher so they do not become more self-absorbed.

Those who have an excessive fear of losing control may be troubled by the idea of meditation. They may have the mistaken idea that meditation is a form of thought or mind control. The goal of merging one's individual consciousness with universal consciousness may be frightening to those who feel insecure and worry about their ability to express their own individuality.

Because meditation allows unconscious thoughts and feelings to rise to the surface for observation by the conscious mind, people with repressed emotions may be temporarily troubled by the experience. Buried memories can emerge that might be disconcerting. This phenomenon is usually mild and temporary and discussion with a meditation teacher, colleague, family member, or therapist may help alleviate this problem.

Part III

Meditation Theory and Philosophy

12. The Mind

In meditation, the mind is studied directly through intense concentration, observation, and introspection. This is in contrast to Western psychology and philosophy, which generally studies the mind by observing external behavior. In meditation, the practitioner develops the ability to observe the functioning and activities of the mind without being distracted or affected by thoughts or emotions.

According to Vedanta philosophy, the mind has several different components. These are *manas, vrittis, buddhi, ahankara,* and *chitta*. Each of these components will affect how human thought occurs. Meditation can transform the thinking process by regulating, adjusting, and strengthening these components of the mind.

Components of the Mind
Manas – Collects data, senses
Vrittis – Thoughts
Buddhi – Decision making
Ahankara – Sense of self, ego
Chitta – Memory, unconscious

Manas is the part of the mind most directly in contact with incoming data from the senses. *Manas* receives, collects, selects, and synthesizes data from the five senses (smell, taste, sight, touch, and sound). It also receives input from the memory and the unconscious. After collecting and organizing the sensory and memory data, thoughts arise (*vrittis*). The *manas* component of the mind then coordinates all the incoming sensory information and associated thoughts with active motor responses. *Manas* responds to this information by force of habit or through primitive instincts or emotions. This function of the mind comes under the influence of the basic urges, including the need for food, shelter, sleep, and sex. If functioning alone, *manas* reacts instinctively and directs an action mechanically. On its own, it cannot make decisions. Intelligent use of all the information available to *manas* depends on the activity of two other functions of the mind, *ahankara* and *buddhi*. Impressions first appear on the mental screen of *manas*, become related to the person's sense of self (*ahankara*), and then a decision can be made (*buddhi*).

Buddhi is the component of the mind responsible for decision-making. *Buddhi* forms a plan based on the core of information received by *manas*. *Buddhi* decides if a person responds to an urge, thought, emotion, or desire and what course of action to take. *Buddhi* is responsible for a person's ability to clearly discriminate right from wrong.

Ahankara is the function of the mind that gives humans self-awareness. It is the sense of "I" that separates awareness of oneself from other people. It is somewhat similar to the idea of "ego" in psychology.

Chitta is similar to the idea of the unconscious in modern psychology, acting as a passive reservoir by receiving and storing information from the senses. *Chitta* also corresponds to the memory, containing impressions of past thoughts and experiences. Emotions often get activated and stimulated from the memories contained in *chitta*.

Meditation has positive effects on each of these components of the mind. Thoughts (*vrittis*) are considered waves of *manas*. Ordinarily, a thought wave arises in the mind, lasts for a few moments and is quickly replaced by another thought. During meditation, a succession of identical thought waves is consciously raised in the mind with such rapidity that no new thought wave can take its place. Perfect continuity of concentration is the ultimate result, with all thoughts fused into one.[12]

Meditation has the effect of slowing sensory impressions and information that can inundate and overwhelm *manas*. During meditation, the thought waves in *manas* are controlled, allowing the mind to rest and become more focused. This allows memories and unconscious impressions from *chitta* to rise to the surface of the conscious mind for internal mental analysis.

Meditation also transforms *buddhi*, allowing for the development of clearer decision-making, such as the ability to more easily disregard distracting impulses that normally flow through *manas*. Decisions are made quickly and effortlessly as we see and understand the implications of our observations and experiences with greater clarity. Meditation helps to develop higher qualities of *buddhi* such as intuition, wisdom, and the ability to reason carefully.

Meditation has important effects on *ahankara*. When practicing meditation, we realize that a strong sense of self is important to differentiate us as unique individuals. Meditation helps us develop a strong inner center, confidence, and a healthy sense of ourselves. At the same time, during meditation we also learn not to be restricted by or overly identified with our own sense of self, which can separate us from other people and the world. Meditation teaches the practitioner to expand the sense of individual self to experience a more unified universal consciousness.

13. *Raja* Yoga: The Integrated Path of Meditation

There are several philosophical and spiritual paths that lead to the development of mental discipline and concentration. The ultimate goals of these paths are the attainment of joy, inner peace, and freedom. Each path involves intense mental focus on a single thought, feeling, or action. This allows the student to concentrate on one thing at a time, helping set the stage for meditation.

The path of devotion and love is called *bhakti* yoga in the Indian schools of philosophy. The Sanskrit word *bhakti* means devotion. When we follow this path, we dedicate ourselves to serving God. We surrender all our mental and physical resources to attain the ultimate reality, expressed through our own idea of divinity. Our emotions are channeled towards feelings of reverence, love, and selfless action. When we practice meditation on this path, we often use images of God or forms of intense prayer as the object of concentration. Certain branches of the Christian faith, especially monastic traditions, Jewish people who follow the path of Hasidic mysticism, and the Sufis in the Islamic religion are examples of people who follow the path of devotion and love.

The path of knowledge is called *jnana* yoga. *Jnana* is a Sanskrit word that is translated as "knowledge" or "intellect." Knowledge of the underlying truths of existence is the goal of this inner path. When following this path, we use our intellect to attain wisdom and to understand the mysteries of life. Questions such as "who am I?" and "what is the meaning of life?" are pondered with great intensity. The ultimate goal of this path is self-realization, where knowledge of our internal states leads to understanding the universe and all its manifestations. Meditation by students on the path of the intellect often begins by contemplating philosophical writings such as the Hindu Vedas and Upanishads, the Koran, the ancient Chinese treatise called the Tao Te Ching, or the Bible. We then let go of all preconceived notions of life and allow our minds to become vessels that can receive true knowledge and understanding.

The path of action and selfless service is called *karma* yoga in the East. The word *karma* means action and refers to the law of cause and effect. This path involves performing all actions with precision and great skill. There is selfless dedication to channeling our mind, body, and speech to either mastering a specific goal or to living life simply and skillfully. Each word, every gesture, and all action have some meaning. The student on the path of *karma* yoga recognizes that for every action taken, there will be a reaction. By being self-disciplined and by performing all the simple tasks of the day with full attention, we generate few reactions. At the same time, we recognize that each action taken is part of the overall harmony of the universe.

Paths of Spirituality
Path of devotion and love - bhakti yoga
Path of knowledge - jnana yoga
Path of action and selfless service - karma yoga
Path of meditation - raja yoga
Path of the primal force - kundalini yoga
Path of sound - mantra yoga
Path of expanded consciousness - tantric yoga

People practicing the path of action and selfless service often work in the healing, teaching, and social services professions. Without ego, these individuals devote their time and energy to help others. Other individuals who follow the path of action are those who devote their entire mind and body to developing a particular art or skill, which represents to them the perfect manifestation of universal harmony. Japanese archery training and tea ceremonies, Sufi rug weaving, martial arts training, and Sufi Dervish and Hasidic dancing are all examples of this.

The path of meditation in the Indian tradition of Samkhya philosophy is called *raja* (royal) yoga. This is perhaps the most systematic path that leads to meditation because it concerns itself with three realms of existence: the physical, mental, and spiritual, and helps us gain mastery of these dimensions. Following this path, we embark on an internal journey from the external body to the innermost parts of consciousness. There are eight steps in the ladder of *raja* yoga and as we climb on one step, we become aware of the next step. When practicing *raja* yoga we learn to systematically prepare ourselves for meditation by first encouraging ethical behaviors and by practicing good health habits. We practice body and breathing exercises to help focus the mind. We learn to control our desires, emotions, thoughts, and subtle impressions that lie dormant in the unconscious. This path of meditation steadies the mind and makes it highly focused and one-pointed, leading to increased awareness and to a more expanded state of consciousness.

Three other paths closely related to *raja* yoga are the path of primal force (*kundalini* yoga), the path of sound (*mantra* yoga), and the path of expanded consciousness (*tantric* yoga). The primary focus of these paths is to intensify the practice of meditation, the seventh step of *raja* yoga. *Kundalini* yoga uses *hatha* yoga postures, *pranayama* techniques, and concentration practices to activate the body's latent energy (*kundalini*) to move to higher centers of consciousness. *Mantra* yoga uses subtle inner vibration and sound (*mantra*) to deepen meditation. *Tantric* yoga focuses on the inner centers of consciousness (*chakras*) in meditation and uses an integrated approach of breathing exercises, *kundalini* activation, and *mantra* to attain expanded states of consciousness.

The *raja* yoga path of meditation is an exact science. It is an inward journey that uses a detailed map as a guide that has been developed over thousands of years. The techniques and benefits gained from this meditative tradition can be verified by anyone who accepts the prescribed methods as a hypothesis and then tests them by his or her own experience. The practices of *raja* yoga and meditation are systematic disciplines that do not impose unquestioning faith but encourage healthy personal decision-making and discrimination.

When we prepare for and practice the form of meditation in this book, we follow the systematic steps of *raja* yoga along with the related paths of *kundalini, mantra*, and *tantric* yoga. The eight rungs on the ladder of the *raja* yoga path of meditation are described below.

Eight Steps of Raja Yoga
Yamas – Regulation
Niyamas – Observances
Asanas – Postures and cleansings
Pranayama – Breathing exercises
Pratyahara – Sense withdrawal
Dharana – Concentration
Dhyana – Meditation
Samadhi – Absorption, Enlightenment

1. *Yama*s are regulations of our relationships with others. These regulations all lead to modification of behavior, replacing negative habits with ethical values. When these restraints are practiced, the student remains free of guilt and remorse and experiences a greater sense of self-confidence, fulfillment, and peace of mind. Regulation of attitudes helps to conserve and direct our energy to higher spiritual practices. The five *yama*s are presented below.

Yamas: Restraints
Non-violence of thought, action, and speech
Truthfulness to oneself and others
Non-stealing
Control of sexual and sensual desires
Non-possessiveness and non-attachment

Non-violence in thought, action, and speech is the first regulation. In Sanskrit, the word for non-violence is *ahimsa*. When we practice non-harming we purposefully avoid hurting another person physically or emotionally, we do not talk behind another person's back, and we are not even too hard on ourselves. It is a similar concept to the Hippocratic Oath when a physician pledges to "first, do no harm." Even if we cannot help another person or our community, we must not cause more pain or suffering in another's life.

Truthfulness to ourselves and to others is the second *yama*. Being truthful allows for the development of trust, inner strength, and courage.

Non-stealing is the third regulation. Both lying and stealing inevitably lead to more deception to cover up the original lie or theft. A great amount of time and energy is wasted in these attempts to cover up misappropriations. Our conscience will often be affected leading to preoccupation with troublesome thoughts.

Control of sensual and sexual desires is the fourth *yama*. Preoccupation with satisfying sexual urges can be very distracting to the spiritual path. Being moderate with our desires, not manipulating another for sexual control, and directing our affection to a mutually agreeable loved one all represent control of the sensual desires.

Non-possessiveness is the fifth regulation. There is a great amount of time wasted in accumulating possessions that are useless or unnecessary in daily life. Attachment to material wealth leads to discontentment because we either worry about what we do not have or fear we will lose what we already do have.

2. *Niyamas* are observances of body and mind and include the following five major principles. These observances enable us to develop self-awareness and self-control and prepare us for more advanced practices.

Cleanliness and purity of body and mind are the first observances. Being clean physically is an easy task to accomplish, but purity of the mind involves attempting to be discriminating and mindful at all times.

Contentment is the second *niyama* and involves creating a state of mind that encourages feelings of tranquility and equilibrium in all circumstances. Learning to be content in life regardless of wealth or personal status is the goal of this observance. Eliminating the desire to accumulate more possessions than is necessary for healthy and comfortable living helps cultivate contentment.

Niyamas: Observances
Cleanliness of body and mind
Contentment and equilibrium
Practices for healthy body and mind
Study of philosophy and inspiring readings
Surrender and devotion to higher consciousness

Practices that bring about health of body and mind are the third observance. This includes using preventive approaches to health care such as good nutrition and exercise.

Study of spiritual readings constitutes the fourth *niyama*. Reading books of philosophy and religion and studying the writings of inspirational spiritual leaders are examples of this observance.

Surrender to the higher self and ultimate reality is the fifth *niyama*. This involves devoting our body, mind, ego, and intellect to the pursuit of knowledge, truth, and wisdom.

3. *Asanas* are postures that include *hatha* yoga poses to ensure physical well-being, strength, and flexibility. While *hatha* yoga postures have many positive health benefits, such as helping back pain, lowering blood pressure, and stimulating under-active glands, the ultimate goal is to help develop a steady, strong spine for meditative practices. *Hatha* yoga practices also include practicing specific body washes and cleansings (*kriyas*), placing the hands and fingers in certain positions to direct internal energy flow (*mudras*), and the application of physical locks (*bandhas*). These physical locks involve compressing and stimulating various glands, nerves, and energy centers (*chakras*). There are also specific sitting postures that allow for effortless, steady, and more lengthy meditation practices. All these *hatha* yoga practices are explained in more detail in chapter 19, *Hatha* Yoga, in chapter 20, Sitting Postures, and in chapter 22, *Kundalini*.

4. *Pranayama*, which means control of *prana* or energy, are breathing exercises that are essential for integrating body, emotions, and mind. They are useful in treating many physical illnesses such as asthma, sinus conditions, digestive problems, and thyroid disorders. They are also helpful for controlling stressful situations and treating emotional problems including anxiety, obsessive-compulsive disorder, and depression. The ability of breathing exercises to affect the mind and emotions can be explained by the fact that there are direct nerve connections from the nose and lungs to the brain with important relays to the nervous

and endocrine (hormone) systems. *Pranayama* techniques are also essential to enhance meditation. The next chapter, *Prana* and the *Nadis*, offers a more detailed definition of *prana* and in chapter 21 in Part IV, called *Pranayama* and Breathing, there are descriptions of the specific breathing exercises associated with *pranayama*.

5. *Pratyahara* is sense withdrawal and control of the five senses (taste, smell, sight, touch, and hearing). We learn to voluntarily draw the senses inward and thus do not allow ourselves to be distracted by the world. Sense withdrawal from external desires and objects is an essential preliminary to deeper concentration and meditative techniques.

6. *Dharana* means concentration and includes practices where the distracted thoughts of the mind are gathered together and directed inwards towards an object of concentration through continual voluntary attention. In Tantric forms of meditation, the objects of concentration are inner sounds and vibrations (*mantras*), visual images and geometric forms (*yantras*), energy centers in the body (*chakras*), breath, and light.

7. *Dhyana* is meditation, which is sustained and unbroken concentration. While concentration techniques make the mind steady and one-pointed, meditation expands the one-pointed mind to a higher state of intuition and awareness by piercing through the conscious and unconscious mind.

8. *Samadhi* is absorption with the object of concentration and meditation (*mantras*, *yantras*, or *chakras*) through intense and prolonged effort. As the focus of concentration deepens, associated sounds and visual images fade. A conscious and calm state ensues, devoid of thought. The sense of self dissolves, replaced by a sense of universal consciousness. This state is free of the limitations of time and space. As the state of *samadhi* deepens, all experiences of duality and separation are lost, and union with the underlying forces of the universe is experienced. At the deepest levels of meditation, there is absorption into universal consciousness. While

it is impossible to adequately verbalize such an experiential state, it has been described as having ultimate wisdom and knowledge, waves of tranquility, a sense of beauty, boundless and transporting joy, and feelings of bliss. A person reaching the state of *samadhi* has continual access to these experiences and at the same time lives simply in the world to help others.[13]

14. *Prana* and the *Nadis*

In meditation and yoga science, *prana* is the energy or life force of humanity. *Prana* is said to flow through various channels called *nadis*. Unlike the bronchial tubes that conduct air or the nerves that transmit electrochemical impulses, *nadis* are not anatomical structures. They exist on a more subtle level and cannot be seen by even the most powerful microscope. The *nadis* are somewhat similar to the meridians that are often described in acupuncture. The *nadis* can be perceived through the continual practice of *pranayama* and meditation when the obstacles of body tension, breathing irregularities, and rapidly changing thoughts are quieted and stilled.

Type of Prana	Location of Prana	Function of Prana
Udana	Throat area	Speech, senses
Samana	Naval area	Digestion, metabolism
Apana	Anal area	Elimination, excretion, urination, exhalation
Prana	Chest area	Inhalation
Vyana	Entire body	Circulation of blood, lymph, nerve impulses

In a larger sense, *prana* may be considered the fundamental active energy of the universe. *Prana* mainly enters the human body through the breath. Once in the body, *prana* flows to different locations and controls specific functions. The five *prana*s are: *udana, samana, vyana, apana,* and *prana* (the latter, though having the same name, also represents one of the subclassifications). *Udana* is located in the area of the throat and is responsible for speech and control of the sensory nerves. *Samana* is located around the center of the abdomen and is responsible for digestion, metabolism, and assimilation. *Vyana* circulates throughout the entire body and is responsible for circulation of blood, lymph, and nerve impulses. *Apana* is located in the area of the anus and bladder and is responsible for elimination, excretion, and urination, as well as the exhalation part of breathing. *Prana* is located in the cardiac and lung region and is responsible for inhalation.

Pranic energy enters the body with the inspired air and immediately flows into the *nadis* located in the nose. Other portals of entry also exist, and as we learn to follow its movement, *prana* can be consciously drawn inwards at various locations such as the *chakras*, which are areas of intense and highly focused energy. Individuals deeply immersed in the practices of meditation say that there are approximately 72,000 *nadis*. Many *nadis* originate in the third *chakra*, located in the solar plexus area. Fourteen of these *nadis* are considered to be of greatest importance. These *nadis* flow and merge into certain concentrated areas such as the *chakras*. If the flow of *pranic* energy through the inspired air is regulated, smooth, and consistent, this is usually associated with good physical and emotional health. Abnormal rhythms are often associated with illness.

Pingala is the *nadi* associated with the right side of the body. It corresponds to active metabolic processes and sympathetic nervous system activity. Yogic meditation symbolism describes *pingala* as being masculine, energizing, and its symbols are the sun and light. As air enters the right nostril, the *prana* is conveyed to *pingala* located within the right nostril.

Ida is the *nadi* connected with the left nostril, the left side of the body, the parasympathetic nervous system, and the receptive and more feminine aspects of human nature. In meditative symbolism, *ida* is associated with darkness and the moon. Both *ida* and *pingala* cross each other as they travel from the nose down and up the body, intersecting within the *chakras*.

Sushumna corresponds to the central axis of the human body and represents the uniting and integration of *pingala* and *ida*. It is said to be located within the spinal cord of the physical body. *Prana* flows through *sushumna* when both nostrils are open and directing the flow of air evenly.

Meditation is most easily practiced when air and *prana* are flowing through *sushumna*. This leads to a relaxed body and a calm and focused mind. There are several breathing techniques that promote the entry of *prana* into *sushumna*. For example, alternate nostril breathing involves physically moving the breath from side to side in the nose with the goal of stimulating *ida* and *pingala*, so that the physical and mental functions associated with each are regulated and balanced. This breathing technique also helps to equalize the flow of breath and *prana* so that *prana* will begin to travel through *sushumna*. When this occurs, the most primal energy called *kundalini* is activated.[14] The subject of *kundalini* is discussed in greater detail in chapter 22, *Kundalini*.

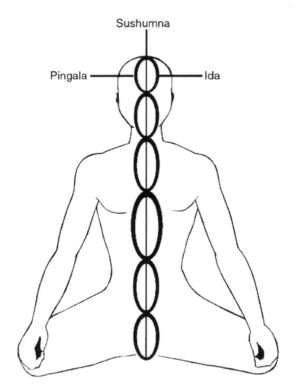

The Main Nadis

15. *Chakras*

Meditation involves focusing the mind on a thought or object. There are some objects of concentration that not only center and calm the mind but also are intrinsically connected to higher states of consciousness and therefore have inherent power to lead the practitioner of meditation to experience these states. These objects of concentration include the *chakras*, *mantras*, and *yantras*.

*Chakra*s are subtle centers within the body where physical, psychological, and spiritual forces interact and intersect. A *chakra*, which means wheel or circle, is seen in a deep meditative state and is experienced as an energy field. As the movement of spokes emanating from a central motionless hub characterizes the wheel, the *chakra*s represent an area of energy surrounding a central point from which motion and energy originate. Each subtle energy wheel represents a force field that transforms energy from its source (consciousness) into various physical, mental, and spiritual qualities.

While these centers are described as being inside the spinal cord and correspond to major nerve plexuses and are associated with anatomical organs and endocrine glands, the *chakra*s cannot be found by dissecting the human body. They can only be experienced and seen by adjusting our internal perception to a higher and subtler frequency. Meditation theory teaches that the symbols associated with the *chakra*s are not simply abstract representations. Just as iron filings form certain patterns reflecting the electromagnetic field of a nearby magnet, the energy that flows from the transforming stations (*chakra*s) of the body also forms particular patterns, reflecting the energy field of that *chakra*. Thus, the symbolism of the heart *chakra* as two intersecting triangles (similar to the Star of David) surrounded by twelve lotus petals actually mirrors the energy formation particular to that area. (See the illustration on the front cover of this book for a pictorial representation of the *chakra*s.) As the energy of the *chakra* continues to send pulsations and vibrations outwards, not only are geometric shapes formed, but specific sounds (*mantras*), colors, senses (smell, taste, touch, sight, and hearing), elements (earth, water, fire, air, and space), and personality characteristics are also manifested.

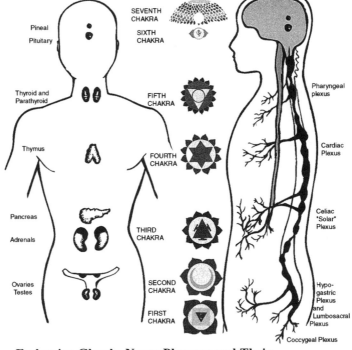

Endocrine Glands, Nerve Plexuses and Their Relationship with the Chakras

The *chakra*s are interconnected by the energy channels (*nadis*) located within and parallel to the spinal column. In the ordinary person, the *chakra*s are functioning at a minimum level and are not harmonized with each other. Meditation theory compares this to a drooping, closed lotus flower. Through intense concentration and inner meditative practices on these energy centers, the *chakra*s become more active, like lotus flowers opening to the sun in full bloom. In meditation, the *chakra*s are increasingly harmonized with each other until they vibrate in unison. When this occurs, the body, emotions, and mind are balanced and higher states of awareness are experienced. The goals of meditating on the seven major *chakra*s are to activate the centers through intense concentration and to stimulate the physical and psycho-spiritual qualities associated with each *chakra* as well as to raise the latent energies from the lower, more physical, *chakra*s to the higher, more spiritually-evolved ones.

Kundalini-shakti, which is discussed in greater depth in chapter 22 is the primal force of the seen and unseen universe and is manifested and expressed within the human through the *chakra*s. As a result of this phenomenon, the individual experiences the world through the particular frame of reference of the individual *chakra*s. Not only do the *chakra*s govern and vitalize the physical functioning of certain areas of the body, but they also correspond to and influence the emotional, psychological, and spiritual qualities associated with the specific region. For example, when the mind and *kundalini* are expressed through the fifth *chakra*, we become creative and communicate effectively. If our mind and energy are primarily expressed through the third *chakra*, then we might experience the world and other people in terms of power and control.

Meditation on the *chakra*s is of fundamental importance in the Tantric systems of meditation. The seven major *chakra*s and three of the most important minor *chakra*s are described below.

Muladhara, which means "foundation," is the first *chakra* and is located at the base of the spine. It is associated with the sacral and pelvic nerve plexuses of the physical body. Associated with the first *chakra* are the physical concerns of bowel functioning as well as the psychological issues of emotional security. Physical problems that are associated with this area are chronic diarrhea, constipation, and irritable bowel syndrome. Psychological issues associated with the first *chakra* relate to the issues of survival and self-preservation. When we are overly focused on this center, we overly identify with physical existence. We might experience life as an intense need to survive at all costs. We may be subject to fear of others and feel separate and alone. A lack of energy in the first *chakra* is associated with feelings of insecurity. Integration at the first *chakra* leads to feelings of security and stability and forms a strong foundation for managing the complexities of life.

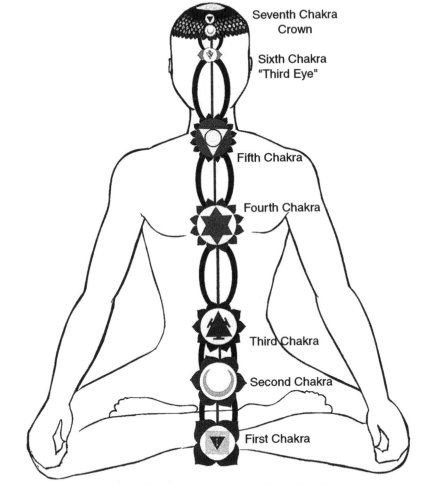

Seventh Chakra
Crown

Sixth Chakra
"Third Eye"

Fifth Chakra

Fourth Chakra

Third Chakra

Second Chakra

First Chakra

The Chakras and the Main Nadis

This *chakra* also is the resting-place of great amounts of latent energy (*kundalini-shakti*). When this energy is activated by yoga practices, breathing exercises, and meditation, the *kundalini* force is directed upward to the higher, more spiritually-evolved centers. See chapter 22, *Kundalini*, for more information on this subject.

Muladhara is visually described as being surrounded by four red lotus petals on a circle. Inside the circle is a yellow square and inside this is an inverted red triangle. Within the triangle is the coiled *kundalini* energy. This resembles a serpent wrapped around itself three and one half times with its head facing upwards into the central canal (*sushumna*). The sound (*bija mantra*) associated with this *chakra* is *LAM* (rhymes with *rum* and *numb* as do all the other *chakra* associated *bija mantras*). The significance of *mantras* will be presented in the next chapter, *Mantras*. The element of the first *chakra* is earth and the associated sense is smell.

Svadisthana, which means "her abode," is the second *chakra* and is located within the spinal column across from and slightly above the genital area. It has a correspondence with the plexus of nerves and glands associated with the sexual organs (ovaries and testes). Issues of urinary function, sexuality, and sensuality are associated with this center. When we are not integrated or are overly focused at this center, we may suffer from genital-urinary problems, lower back pain, or be overly involved with seeking sensual pleasures, especially sexual gratification. While desiring pleasure, we will often find the experiences fleeting and insufficient. Other people, especially the opposite sex, are experienced as being simultaneously alluring and to be feared. When there is a lack of energy at this center, we may experience inhibition of sexual expression or have an absence of desire. Integration at the second *chakra* is associated with having the capacity to express both masculine and feminine traits and to have and enjoy healthy, honest, and appropriately directed adult sexual relationships.

Svadisthana is visually described as being surrounded by six dark red (vermilion) lotus petals resting upon a circle. Inside the circle is the color white with a silver crescent moon resting near the bottom. The sound (*bija mantra*) associated with this *chakra* is *VAM*. The element of the second *chakra* is water and the associated sense is taste.

Manipura, which means "filled with jewels," is the third *chakra* and is located across from the navel within the spinal cord. It is associated with the celiac plexus of nerves, the adrenal glands, and the pancreas. This area is also often referred to as the solar plexus. This is the center where energy from the two lower *chakra*s is transformed and stored. Asian martial arts describe this center as being the storehouse of power. Anyone who has ever been punched in the center of the abdomen can testify how it knocks the energy and breath out of them. On a physical level, a lack of energy here can lead to stomach and digestive illnesses. Psychologically, this is the center of ego and competitiveness. There are issues of power over other people, of dominance and submissiveness, and of a need to expand our sphere of influence. The need to prove oneself and gain financial wealth and power are predominant. Anorexia and bulimia are two emotional disorders associated with problems of the third *chakra*. Healthy integration associated with this *chakra* allows for striking a balance between being active and assertive when necessary and being receptive or passive if indicated. There is a desire for success as well as an acceptance of failure.

Those of us who experience life through the third *chakra* tend to be motivated by the desire for external recognition, fame, power, and material wealth. We experience pride and ambition and physical strength and beauty are important to us. We may be demanding of other people's attention and may try to control their actions and beliefs. We often have fiery and powerful personalities.

Manipura is visually described as being surrounded by ten dark blue lotus petals resting on a circle. Inside the circle is a red triangle that is pointed down but which inverts to point upwards during meditation. The sound associated with this *chakra* is *RAM*. The element of the third *chakra* is fire and the associated sense is sight.

Anahata, which means "unheard sound," is the fourth *chakra* and is located across from the heart within the spine and is associated with the cardiac plexus of nerves. Just as the blood from the heart and the oxygen from the lungs sustain the body and a mother's breast milk nurtures her infant, the heart *chakra*, also located in the center of the chest, is associated with the capacity for us to emotionally and spiritually nurture others. On a physical level, imbalances here are associated with lung and heart diseases. A lack of integration at the heart center is psychologically associated with apathy or an inability to offer love to others. Feelings of love and compassion are experienced at this center and giving to others, compassion, selfless love, and empathy are characteristics of a healthy concentration of energy at this center.

Those of us who are able to experience life through the fourth *chakra* practice loving kindness and develop a deeper capacity for expressing love, generosity, forgiveness, and compassion. We become a greater source of inspiration to others and people feel at peace in our presence. We learn to have a greater faith in life and become more optimistic, friendly, patient, and secure. We live life with grace and dignity and are generally respected by our community.

Anahata is visually described as being surrounded by twelve deep red lotus petals resting on a circle. Inside the circle are two blue-green triangles that intersect, one pointed down and the other pointed up. Some people refer to this shape as the Star of David. Inside the six-pointed star is a dark area, often described as a black cave. Inside the cave is a lit candle with a flame that does not flicker. This flame is often described as a reflection of the soul. The soul can be thought of as the eternal and nonchanging Center of Consciousness which channels the energy and creative forces of the universe through the individual. (More information on the Center of Consciousness can be found in chapter 18, *Koshas*: The Five Levels of Consciousness and Holistic Medicine.) The sound (*bija mantra*) associated with this *chakra* is *YAM*. The element of the fourth *chakra* is air and the associated sense is touch.

Hrit is a lesser-known *chakra* closely associated with, connected to, and located slightly below the *anahata chakra*. Great depths of emotion and feelings of devotion are associated with this center. It is described as being surrounded by eight gold lotus petals resting on a circle. Inside the circle is another circle red in color and inside this is an orange circle.

Vishuddha, which means "purified," is the fifth *chakra* and is located across from the throat within the cervical portion of the spinal cord. It is associated with the cervical nerve plexus as well as the nerves of the voice box and with the thyroid gland. Creativity, receptivity to others, and the ability to be nurtured and guided by an inner higher consciousness are qualities associated with the fifth *chakra*. Poor metabolism and thyroid diseases stem from problems with integration at this center and respiratory and throat problems can also occur. Psychologically, we may have difficulty communicating verbally with others, and creative people such as artists may be unable to produce quality work. An integrated focus of energy at this center is associated with being able to trust others, devotion, creativity, and with the capacity to evolve. The ideas of being receptive to and surrendering to our own higher creative instincts are spiritual qualities of this center. The element of the fifth *chakra* is space and the associated sense is hearing.

Those of us who experience life through the fifth *chakra* develop a melodious voice, a good command of speech, the ability to write well, the capacity to understand spiritual writings, and the ability to interpret the deeper significance of dreams.

Vishuddha is described as being surrounded by sixteen dark purple lotus petals resting on a circle. Inside the circle is dark blue in color and in the center is a white circle resting within a white triangle. This is described as the full moon seen against a blue sky. The sound (*bija mantra*) associated with this center is *HAM*. The element of the fifth *chakra* is space and the associated sense is hearing.

Ajna, which means "command," is the sixth *chakra* and is located across from the area between the two eyebrows. It is located near the pineal and pituitary glands deep within the brain. There are also interconnections with the naso-ciliary plexus of the physical nervous system. The center is associated with the psychological and spiritual qualities of intuition, wisdom, and clarity of vision. It is also called the third eye and the eye of insight because it sees inwards into the conscious and unconscious mind. Disorders of integration at this center lead to confusion and potentially serious mental illness. When the *kundalini* energy rises to this level and resides there permanently, a person experiences the highest states of consciousness.

Ajna is described as being surrounded by two light blue lotus petals resting upon a white circle. This has an appearance of an eye. Inside the circle is a small white triangle pointed down. The sound associated with this center is the universal *mantra OM* (rhymes with "home"). The element of the sixth *chakra* is pure mind and it is beyond any sense association.

Indu (also called *soma*) is a minor *chakra* located above the *ajna chakra*. It is said to be the source of a sweet nectar (*soma*) that drips down with the cerebral spinal fluid from the third ventricle of the brain into the spinal cord. When we experience higher states of consciousness, the nectar is tasted in the throat. This *chakra* is visually described as being surrounded by sixteen light blue lotus petals resting on a circle. Inside the circle is a silver-white crescent moon.

Guru is another lesser-known but very important *chakra* located above the *ajna* and *indu chakra*s and below the *sahasrara chakra* (see the description below). It is located at the back of the cerebral cortex part of the brain. It is associated with finely heard *mantras* and sublime images of great luminosity. Meditating on this *chakra* and establishing consciousness here is associated with attainment of great spiritual knowledge and feelings of bliss. This *chakra* is visually described as being surrounded by twelve red lotus petals resting on a circle. Inside the circle is a red inverted triangle.

Sahasrara, which means "thousand petals," is the seventh and highest *chakra* and is associated with the cerebral cortex of the brain. When *kundalini* reaches this level, the individual self merges and is absorbed into universal consciousness. Here there is no distinction between the knower and the known, and there is only perfect knowing.

Sahasrara is described as appearing like one thousand lotus petals of pure light emanating like an umbrella or crown from the top of the head. At times during meditation the crown *chakra* can be visualized as though it is arranged in the variegated colors of the rainbow. All sounds, elements, and senses are absorbed and integrated into the seventh *chakra*.[15]

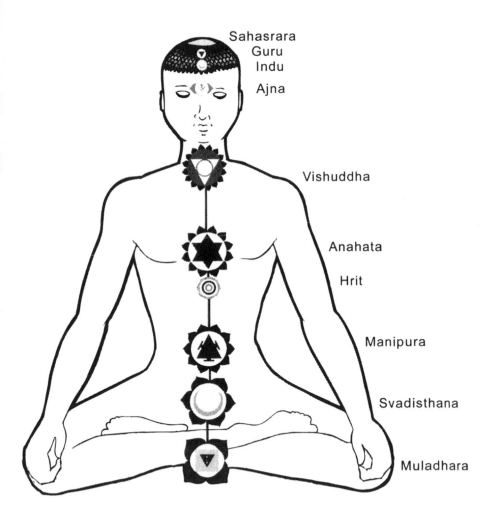

Sahasrara
Guru
Indu
Ajna

Vishuddha

Anahata

Hrit

Manipura

Svadisthana

Muladhara

Seven Major and Three Minor Chakras

Chakra Associations

Chakra	Nerve Association	Gland Association	Physical Quality	Physical Illness
Muladhara	Sacral and pelvic nerves Coccygeal plexus		Bowel function	Irritable bowel syndrome
Svadisthana	Hypogastric plexus Lumbar-sacral plexus	Sexual organ Testes Ovaries	Reprod-uction Sexuality	STD's Urinary tract infections
Manipura	Celiac plexus	Adrenal Pancreas	Diges-tion	Ulcers Indigestion Diabetes
Hrit	Cardiac plexus			
Anahata	Cardiac plexus	Thymus	Breath Circul-ation	Asthma Heart disease
Vishuddha	Pharyngeal plexus	Thyroid Parathyroid	Metabo-lism Speech	Low thyroid function URI's
Ajna	Mid brain	Pineal Pituitary		
Indu	Brain			
Guru	Brain			
Sahasrara	Cerebral cortex of the brain			

Chakra Associations

Psychological & Spiritual Quality	Psycho-logical & Spiritual Problem	Color & Shape of Yantra	Color & No. of Lotus Petals	Sense & Element	Mantra
Strong foundation Security *Kundalini*	Survival Fear Paranoia Insecurity	Yellow square Red triangle	Red & Four	Smell & Earth	LAM
Healthy sexual expression	Sexual concerns	Silver crescent moon	Red & Six	Taste & Water	VAM
Sense of self Power Ego Dominance & submissiveness	Inferiority complex Anorexia	Red triangle	Blue & Ten	Sight & Fire	RAM
Love Devotion		Red circle Orange circle	Gold & Eight		
Compassion Loving kindness	Apathy Grief Hatred	Blue-green Star of David	Red & Twelve	Touch & Air	YAM
Receptivity Communication Creativity	Inhibition of speech and creativity	White moon on blue sky	Purple & Sixteen	Hearing & Space	HAM
Intuition Wisdom Insight		White circle with OM symbol	Blue & Two	Pure mind	OM
Bliss Taste of nectar		Silver crescent moon	Blue & Sixteen		
Sublime *mantras* and vibrations		Red triangle	Red & Twelve		
Enlightenment Highest consciousness		Pure light Rainbow lotus petals	Pure light & 1000		

16. *Mantras*

The word *mantra* is a Sanskrit word composed of the root *man* meaning "to think" and *tra* meaning "instrument to liberate us from bondage." Thus, the word means "an instrument of thought that can free us from the constraints of our mind."

According to Vedanta and Tantric philosophy, consciousness is single, unified, and complete. Consciousness is the intelligent underlying force of the universe and has the inherent desire and the ability to know and experience itself. To become aware, consciousness needs to become differentiated from one into many, so that the many can know the one. The first manifestation of this differentiation is vibration. Human beings experience this vibration in the form of subtle sounds called *mantra*. This infinite vibration is heard only in deep meditation, when the senses and the mind are quieted. Thus, when humans listen for and experience this vibration, they are actually hearing the faint echoes of underlying universal undifferentiated consciousness as it manifests into form.

The theory of consciousness differentiating from one into many is similar to the Big Bang concept of the origin of the universe described in modern physics and cosmology. According to this model, if we were to travel back in time to the very beginning of the universe, we would find that the universe was smaller, hotter, and denser the farther back in time we went. In the very beginning, all forces, matter, and energy were unified in one singular, undifferentiated point of infinite mass and potentiality. When the inner forces of this single infinitesimally small point became intense enough, it exploded, eventually expanding and differentiating into the universe as we now know it. This explosion, called the Big Bang, occurred billions of years ago and can still be heard today by giant earth-based radio telescopes and orbiting satellites. In this sense, the Big Bang echoes all around us, described by physicists and astronomers as cosmic background microwave radiation. Often referred to as the hum of the Big Bang, this subtle noise is almost identical to the idea of the vibration and sound of *mantra*.

We are presently in the expansion stage of the Big Bang. As the expansion continues and the distances between the objects of the universe increase, eventually the gravitational forces holding the objects of the universe together will become weaker. This will lead the universe to collapse in upon itself, with the implosion ultimately resulting in the Big Crunch when the universe again becomes a single infinitely concentrated point. This expansion and contraction of the cosmos will theoretically continue forever. In the meditative traditions this is referred to as the eternal breath of Brahman. Brahman means universal consciousness in Vedanta philosophy or God in the Jewish and Christian religions. God's inhalation corresponds to the expansion phase of the universe and God's exhalation correlates to the contraction phase.

Because *mantras* are an expression of a more complete, unified state, they are uniquely linked to an expanded level of consciousness. *Mantras* help to focus the mind on a single thought and, through consistent practice, they also replace distracting conscious thoughts and disturbing memories from the subconscious. Constant repetition of the *mantra* and listening to its sound gradually pull individual consciousness towards the universal.

In deep meditation ancient practitioners have described hearing subtle sound vibrations. *Mantras* are actually condensed forms or seeds of that vibration experience. Being a seed, it can be nurtured to grow into the entire experience. These *mantras* have been passed on through a long line of teachers. It has been recognized that teachers are simply acting as transmitters, first picking up the sounds and then distributing them to receptive students. The *mantra* itself may be a small word, but being a seed, it has a very powerful effect because of its latent force.[16]

There are several types of *mantras*. *Bija mantras* are sometimes assigned by teachers to initiate their students into the practice of meditation. *Bija mantras* are chosen by meditation teachers based on the personality and life circumstances of their students. Therefore, the *mantra* can be used not only to help focus concentration but also to help the student with specific difficulties. The teacher selects the *mantra* similar to a physician prescribing a medication, except in this case the diagnosis and prescription are made on the spiritual level. The following eight *mantras* are the most common and powerful *bija mantras* recommended by teachers for students to use during their meditations.

1. *AIM* (pronounced "I'm") is the syllable for teacher.
2. *HREEM* (rhymes with "cream") is the syllable for energy.
3. *KLEEM* is the syllable for desire.
4. *KREEM* is the syllable for union.
5. *SHREEM* is the syllable for delight.
6. *TREEM* is the syllable for fire.
7. *STREEM* is the syllable for peace.
8. *HLEEM* is the syllable for protection.[17]

Another type of *bija mantra* is the syllable that corresponds to each of the five lower *chakras*. Beginning at the first *chakra* and moving upwards, the sounds are *LAM, VAM, RAM, YAM,* and *HAM* (each of these sounds rhymes with the word rum or numb). By meditating on the visual image (*yantra*) of each *chakra* and at the same time repeating or listening for the seed *mantra*, the student activates the physical, psychological, and spiritual energies of that *chakra*.[18]

The *mantra SO HAM* is the special universal breath *mantra* that corresponds to the quiet sounds of breathing. *SO* is mentally repeated on inhalation and *HAM* is repeated when breathing out. *HAM SA* is a very similar *mantra* with the *HAM* pronounced on exhalation and *SA* said on inspiration.

The *mantra OM* (rhymes with "home") is the one sound in particular that is considered to be the manifestation of the universal vibration in its most subtle and most sublime form. This *mantra* most closely reflects the initial separation of universal consciousness into the manifest universe. *OM* is the source word that contains all sounds and vibration. It is the mother of all *mantras*. It is considered to be the vibration from which all manifestation comes. By concentrating on the sound of *OM*, the manifesting process is reversed, re-collecting the scattering of energy back towards the source or center where unity is experienced. The *mantra OM* is most closely associated with the sixth *chakra* and is also used in meditation while moving concentration up the *chakras*.

The vibration *OM* can be heard when the mind is calm in deep meditation, reverberating through our minds and the universe around us. *OM* is the primordial sound of timeless consciousness, vibrating within us from the beginningless past. The sound is approximated when putting your ear up to a seashell, or trying to talk with your lips closed. Almost all religious and spiritual traditions have a close form of this sound in its prayer or meditations. In both Christianity and Judaism, prayers end in the word Amen, which approximates the sound of *OM*. In Hinduism, when Sanskrit is used, *OM* is chanted at the beginning of most prayers and rituals. In Islam, prayer often ends in *AMEEN*. In Jewish meditation, the word for peace is *SHALOM* and is often used as a *mantra* in meditation. *SHALOM* is often coordinated with the flow of the breath, with the *SHA* internally repeated on inhalation and the *LOM* silently said on exhalation. The *L* sound quickly becomes silent with the long and gentle exhalation focused on the *OM* sound.[19]

There are four ways to use *mantras* in meditation. The first way is to repeat the sound out loud. Especially when using *OM* as their *mantra,* beginning students of meditation may want to verbally repeat *OM* on three consecutive deep exhalations to become familiar with its tone, rhythm, and vibration. The second way is to whisper the *mantra* under the breath. The third way is to mentally repeat the sound. This can be coordinated with the breath. The fourth way is to simply listen for the sounds and vibration of the *mantra* if the practitioner seems to experience the *mantra* resonating deep within. The latter two methods are encouraged for use in the meditation presented in this book.

When continually repeated, the *mantra* will begin to rise up into conscious awareness on its own, sometimes seeming to call to the person who is meditating. After living with the *mantra* for several years, the student will learn to appreciate its latent and transforming power.

Meditation on the *mantra* ultimately leads us to awareness of the underlying unity of all things and at the same time teaches us to express the manifestation of this oneness in creative ways. Meditation with *mantra* leads us through inner spaces of consciousness, helping us retrace our path to oneness and teaching us to live with the knowledge and joy of what we discover.

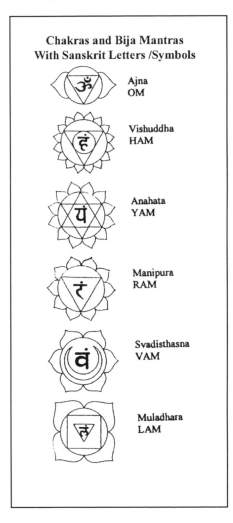

Chakras and Bija Mantras
With Sanskrit Letters /Symbols

Ajna
OM

Vishuddha
HAM

Anahata
YAM

Manipura
RAM

Svadisthasna
VAM

Muladhara
LAM

17. *Yantras*

The term *yantra* derives from the Sanskrit root word *yam* and literally means "a device or instrument that sustains or supports the energy inherent in a particular element, object, or concept." In its application to meditation, *yantra* is an abstract geometric design that functions to support and enhance focus of the mind and to increase inner awareness. A *yantra* represents a drastically reduced image of consciousness. The *yantra* arrangement also reflects the underlying organization of the physical universe as well as the underlying order of both the conscious and unconscious mind. It is a graphic representation of the energies of the universe as these energies manifest into visual form.

In a sense, a *yantra* is a mathematical symbol of consciousness in geometric form. The shapes of these building blocks are mostly simple geometric forms, including points, lines, triangles, squares, rectangles, pentagons, circles, and spirals. These simple shapes are seen even in the smallest physical particles such as molecules, atoms, electrons, and other subatomic structures. Another simple shape also considered a *yantra* is the pictorial shape of the lotus petal, such as the patterns that surround the *chakra*s.

Specific letters are another very important *yantra*, most notably the letters found in Sanskrit and Hebrew. The letters associated with these great languages are not merely used as building blocks for developing spoken and written words. They also represent the sounds, vibrations, and form that ancient spiritually evolved practitioners heard and saw in deep meditation. Thus, using the letter *yantras* in meditation is of paramount importance because they are manifestations of universal consciousness and their internal repetition and visualization lead the mind back to the ultimate source.

The *chakra*s are a special kind of *yantra* because each energy center has a specific geometric form and color. Lotus petal-shaped forms surround all the *chakra*s and internally they have various configurations of lines, circles, crescents, triangles, and spirals. Inside each *chakra*, there is a small *yantra* associated with a Sanskrit letter.

The *Shri Yantra* is considered to be the most perfect representation of how the human being reflects the underlying forces of the universe. Its complex mathematical and geometric structure represents a map of the union of the opposing but complementary forces in the cosmos, including male and female, expansion and contraction, and positive and negative energy. Meditation on this *yantra* is very complex and is associated with *mantra* recitation when visualizing the shapes and patterns. The *Shri Yantra* leads the student to experience and energize the nine *chakra*s (the seven major *chakra*s and the two minor *chakra*s located between the sixth and seventh *chakra*s). Learning to meditate on the *Shri Yantra* is considered to be the most advanced practice in the Samaya path of Tantra philosophy. A highly skilled teacher is needed to guide the student in this meditative practice.[20]

Shri Yantra

18. *Koshas*: The Five Levels of Consciousness and Holistic Medicine

Unlike the Western conception of the human as an amalgam of body and mind, meditation theory recognizes five levels of consciousness that span a much larger spectrum of human experience. The five levels of consciousness are conceptualized as existing from gross external levels to more subtle internal ones, the outer being more dense and obscuring the finer, less material inner layers. Associated with each level is a specific type of awareness. These five levels of consciousness are called sheaths (*koshas*) because of their concentric arrangement, although they all interpenetrate each other. The five major sheaths of consciousness are the body or physical sheath, the energy or breath sheath, the mind sheath, the intellectual or unconscious sheath, and the blissful or transcendental sheath. Within the last sheath lies the Center of Consciousness, the source of all the other levels.

The Center of Consciousness is often compared to light and the different sheaths as lampshades that cover it. Each concentrically placed sheath obscures and conceals the clarity and brilliance of the underlying light source. The shades reflect the light to different degrees and are made of different materials, shapes, and colors. The outermost sheaths are the densest, allowing the least amount of light to penetrate. Those who identify only with the most external sheaths, such as the body, remain oblivious to the more inner levels of consciousness and the Center of Consciousness. They experience life only on a mundane physical level and cannot feel the deeper, more spiritual aspects of their existence. On the other hand, meditation teaches the student to penetrate the sheaths so that he/she can experience the complexity and subtleness of life and more clearly see the source of the inner light.[21]

These sheaths form a continuum, and all levels are interdependent, interconnected, and coordinated closely. Humans exist simultaneously on all these levels. The connections between the levels are maintained by the *chakra*s, as these centers integrate the physical, electromagnetic, mental, and spiritual energies from the various sheaths of consciousness. In this way, body affects mind, breathing affects the unconscious, and the deeper spiritual levels affect all the other levels. Thus, each *kosha* and *chakra* center offers a particular frame of reference through which the individual relates to and experiences the world.

The theoretical construct of the sheaths of consciousness helps explain how the body, mind, and emotions interact in both health and disease. The paradigm of the *koshas* is a very useful medical model because it says that humans exist on several levels, including the physical, energy, conscious mind, unconscious mind, and super conscious mind. If humans exist on these levels, it follows that disease also occurs on these levels and that diagnosis and treatment can be focused at the appropriate level. Thus, the philosophy of the sheaths represents a model of preventive and holistic medicine which offers both conceptual theory and pragmatic treatment approaches into which various conventional and alternative therapeutic systems of health care can be organized and integrated.

The body sheath is the first and outermost layer and is called the *annamaya kosha*. *Anna* means "food" and *maya* means "illusion." Thus, *annamaya kosha* refers to the physical body (which is made of food) and represents the densest level of illusion that obscures consciousness. This *kosha* includes the anatomical and physical structure of the human body. Traditional methods used to treat people who have problems on this level are diet, vitamins, minerals, drugs, physical therapy, and surgery. Complementary and alternative approaches include more broad-based nutrition and supplementation, herbal medicine, and body therapies such as massage, *hatha* yoga, martial arts, and tai chi. People involved with meditation often simplify their diets, moving towards eating less meat, fat, and refined sugar, all of which help to decrease the risk of heart disease, cancer, and hypertension. They learn to be observant as to what foods create clarity of mind, energize the body, create mental dullness, or cause irritability, stuffiness, or gas. Yoga, martial arts, and other forms of exercise are often practiced because of their positive effects on mind-body awareness and integration.

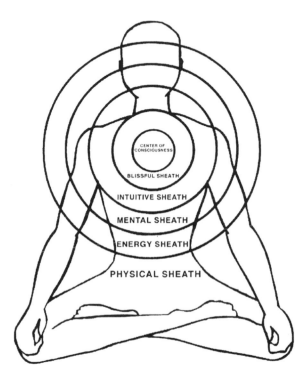

The Koshas: The Sheaths of Consciousness

    The energy sheath is the second layer and is called the *pranayama kosha*. This *kosha* consists of the subtle forces of *prana*, which means "energy," and is sustained and nourished by the breath. There are really no approaches in traditional allopathic medicine that either diagnose or treat a patient on this level, mainly because conventional perspectives do not really recognize the existence of this level. Holistic approaches that treat the energy sheath are biofeedback, acupuncture, *pranayama* (breathing) exercises, and homeopathy. With respect to the human organism, energy has various names and forms. Chinese call energy *chi* and homeopathic physicians call it the vital force. In all traditions, it is considered the life force that animates the human organism. The major transmitter of energy from the external world to the individual is through breathing and, to a lesser extent, food.

Meditation theory suggests that because energy (second sheath) links body (first and outermost sheath) and mind (third sheath), imbalances on the energy level often reflect or predate physical disorders or emotional problems. Before mental disease can produce physiologic changes, the disharmony first may pass through the intermediary energy level. Conversely, suppressed physical illnesses may show manifestations in energy patterns before affecting the mind or emotions.

Acupuncture works on the energy level by needles or finger pressure being applied to pathways that transmit energy flow. These pathways are called meridians and have no real correlation with nerve pathways. They are similar to the *nadis* of meditation theory. By stimulating certain points, a balancing of energy flow is facilitated in distant organs. Pain reduction and anesthesia are also possible through acupuncture therapy.

When there are uneven patterns of breathing, the flow of energy through the body is also affected. Physiologically, irregular breathing influences every cell of the body by its effect on oxygenation and blood flow, on the central nervous system, and the autonomic nervous system. By consciously controlling the breath, we learn to modulate and direct the amount and quality of energy entering the body. Through slow and deliberate practice of simple breathing exercises, such as diaphragmatic breathing, we learn to discern which irregularities of the breath flow reflect particular illnesses, how certain states of mind adversely affect breathing patterns, and also how to redirect and guide the breath to create harmony between the mind and body.

Homeopathy is an interesting form of medicine that acts directly on the energy level, which is called the vital force.

Through the process of dilution and vigorous shaking, which is also called attenuation or potentization, the medicines are prepared and refined in such a way that they work on an energy level. The medicine, which is called a remedy in homeopathy, is offered to the patient when it matches the energy level of the illness. This has the effect of catalyzing a healing response of the body and mind.

The mental sheath is the third layer and is called the *manomaya kosha*. *Mano* means "mind" and this level corresponds to the conscious mind. This sheath helps make up our personalities and is sustained through active thought. Treatment modalities that act on this level include various Western psychotherapies, especially those approaches that are behavioral in orientation. Through careful observation and analysis, the patient learns to identify his problems and then forms strategies to solve them. Various medications to control depression, anxiety, or bipolar disease also directly affect mental functioning. Relaxation and concentration techniques associated with the meditative traditions also directly affect conscious mental activity. By emphasizing non-attached observation of the flow of thoughts, we learn to clear the conscious mind by letting go of distracting and habitual thoughts and emotions. By mentally sending messages to our body and by observing the breath and energy flow, we can learn to relax muscular tension and help better regulate tension-related diseases such as high blood pressure and migraine headaches.

The intuitive sheath is the fourth layer and is called the *vijnanamaya kosha*. *Vijnana* refers to the intuitive knowledge of consciousness and this level corresponds to some degree with the Western idea of the unconscious mind. Areas of mental health care associated with this sheath are the techniques of free association in Freudian psychoanalysis, dream analysis of Jungian psychology, and certain meditative practices. All therapies directed to this level help us become aware of unconscious motivations and emotions as well as refine our intuitive, nonverbal faculties. This allows for integration of deeper, unexplored levels of the human psyche within us.

Meditation helps problems that arise from the intuitive sheath by teaching us to witness troublesome thought and emo-

101

tional patterns. Through meditation we begin to realize the fleeting, ever-changing character of the mind. Acknowledging the impermanence of thought brings awareness that there is an element of unreality associated with patterns of the mind. We come to know a quiet, calm, and centered part of ourselves that lies beyond the mind. We can then observe the mind and use it as a tool, yet not become identified with it. When practicing meditation we learn to let go of transient desires and vacillating emotions. We become less attached to meaningless mental events, freeing mental energy for more creative purposes and expanded awareness.

The blissful sheath is the fifth layer and is called the *anandamaya kosha*. *Ananda* means "bliss" and this sheath corresponds with higher states of consciousness. The only approaches that can apply to this level are more advanced meditation techniques that help create a state of inner peace, harmony, deep understanding, compassion, love, and feelings of bliss. With sustained concentration on a single object, especially a sound (*mantra*), the practitioner can become absorbed with the sound, and is led inwards towards the Source/Center of Consciousness.

The Center of Consciousness lies within the fifth and innermost sheath and is considered to be the source of all the other sheaths of consciousness. It is that part of the individual (self) that is most intimately connected with the universal (Self). When meditation leads a person to the Center of Consciousness, the narrow confining ego (sense of self) is cast off, and one merges with the source of all consciousness, which is within all humans and is nonchanging and eternal. It is described as a place of complete knowledge, absolute peace, indescribable joy, and ultimate bliss. The meditative process finally culminates with the elimination of mundane distractions and absorption with the source of consciousness. We become fully awake and live beyond the bondage of time, space, and causation. This state has many names, including *samadhi*, *nirvana*, the Tao, God consciousness, Christ consciousness, enlightenment, or self-realization.[22]

Part IV

Preparing for Meditation

19. *Hatha* Yoga

The word *hatha* is composed of two smaller words. *Ha* means "sun" and *tha* means "moon." The word yoga means "to unite." Thus, *hatha* yoga means "to unite the sun and moon." The goal of practicing *hatha* yoga for men and women is to unite the qualities associated with the sun, such as the right side, warmth, activity, and masculinity, with the qualities associated with the moon, such as the left side, coolness, passivity, and feminine. This merging of the two polar opposites results in the birth of higher consciousness.

The exercises and practices of *hatha* yoga are part of the third step on the path of *raja* yoga. *Hatha* yoga practices include a series of physical movements and postures (*asanas*), body cleansings (*kriyas*), and certain anatomical locks (*bandhas*). *Asanas* and *kriyas* are discussed in this chapter and *bandhas* are described in greater detail in chapter 22, *Kundalini*. While the ultimate purpose of *hatha* yoga is to create a strong and stable body so the practitioner can sit for longer and more comfortable meditation sessions, there are also important health benefits associated with the various techniques.

On a physical level, *hatha* yoga techniques offer a systematic method of purifying and strengthening the body through the practice of various stretching postures that enable a person to become graceful, relaxed, and supple. *Hatha* yoga postures also work to enhance balance and symmetry of the left and right sides of our body and to promote equilibrium between the sympathetic and parasympathetic nervous systems. This is accomplished by alternating standing postures with inverted postures and forward bending *asanas* with backward bending poses, as well as practicing twisting postures first on one side and then switching to the other side. Because the poses cause gentle compression of the internal organs, digestive functioning often improves and under-active endocrine glands are stimulated. Large and small muscles relax as a result of practicing *hatha* yoga *asanas* and this can be of benefit for illnesses that are associated with abnormal muscular contraction such as high blood pressure, headaches, and asthma.

To understand how the practices of *hatha* yoga help the body and mind and prepare the student for meditation, it is important to describe the interconnection between the brain and the muscular-skeletal system. The areas of the brain responsible for maintaining muscle tone are located deep within the brain. These areas, which are referred to as the lower primitive brain centers, were the first to develop as the brain evolved and are controlled without our conscious direction. These reflexes are modified by input from the conscious part of our brain, the cerebral cortex. The cortex is the latest part of our brain to evolve and is considered to be the higher brain center.

In the most natural state, the more primitive lower brain center helps maintain a relaxed supple body. As we age, however, our conscious concerns and desires begin to interfere with the normal maintenance of relaxed muscle tone.

The proper practice of *hatha* yoga allows the primitive unconscious lower brain centers to adjust muscle tone unimpeded by inhibiting thoughts. This is done by assuming different *asanas*, which leads to activation of certain reflexes that are integrated in the lower brain centers and normally function without conscious awareness. It is through these reflexes that normal tone is reestablished. The postures used are, in a sense, also primitive in that they mimic the positions of animals, as is reflected in their names, including the butterfly, dog, peacock, cobra, or locust. Perhaps these postures facilitate a regression to the evolutionary roots of human beings, where posture is not distorted by conflicts of the conscious mind. To ensure that the lower brain centers are free from conscious cerebral inhibitory control, the mind is focused on the breath. Free from the conscious influence, the lower centers can reestablish proper muscle tone through the natural adjusting reflexes initiated by the *hatha* yoga postures.

To gain the maximum benefit from the *hatha* yoga *asanas*, it is best to relax deeply while doing the postures, to breathe evenly and slowly, and to focus on the area of stretch. The postures should be held with little movement and when coming out of the postures, it should be done slowly and gently. When *hatha* yoga postures are done for health purposes or in preparation for meditation, the following sequence is recommended: stretching exercises, standing postures, backward-bending postures, forward-bending poses, twisting postures, inverted postures, relaxation techniques, and breathing exercises. (See pages 110-111 for pictures of some commonly practiced *asanas*.)

When beginning the *asanas*, we should be receptive, patient, and calm. It is generally best to practice regularly, at the same time daily. Two excellent times to practice are early mornings after going to the bathroom and taking a warm shower. This will help us feel calm before meeting the challenges of our daily life. Doing yoga at night will help reduce the tension accumulated during the day and help allow for a restful sleep. When practicing *asanas*, *pranayama*, or meditation, it is best to wear loose fitting clothes and practice in a quiet, draft free room. We should wait two to four hours after eating to begin and should always relieve the bladder and bowels before commencing the postures. It is generally recommended that women who are menstruating refrain from doing the more strenuous postures, but meditation can always be practiced. While some mild discomfort may occur when we stretch tense muscles, we should maintain awareness not to stretch beyond our capacity to avoid injury. We should ease up on the poses if we feel burning pains or have involuntary shaking.

The manner in which we practice *hatha* yoga determines the quality of the benefits we will experience. A systematic program should be followed, allowing for gradual perfecting of the postures and incorporating the progressive development of the following qualities: flexibility, balance, strength, and stillness. In general, the beginner should endeavor to develop each of these qualities in this order, achieving a certain level of proficiency in each one before attempting the next. For example, if we are just starting to practice the *asanas*, we should initially practice gentle stretching exercises, which are designed to increase flexibility and mobility of the body, thus laying the foundation for the development of balance. A stretch in one direction is balanced by a stretch in the opposite direction. Only after we have attained a certain degree of flexibility and balance should we attempt postures that involve greater strength and power. As we work to enhance flexibility, balance, and strength, it is essential to establish a smooth and even rhythm to the flow of the breath and to coordinate the breath with the movements. As muscle tension is released, the flow of energy and *prana* are also unblocked. With continued practice of regulation of breathing coordinated with the postures, there is a balancing of the two branches of the autonomic nervous system, leading to state of relaxation, calmness, and inner stillness.

Because of these relaxing effects, *hatha* yoga is also helpful on an emotional level. While doing the physical postures, the release of muscle tension not only results in increased flexibility but also helps to liberate pent-up emotions and conflicts that created or underlies the original body tension. Working through or letting go of physical resistance can trigger a concomitant response on the emotional level, liberating the person from the subjective feeling of restriction.

Hatha yoga also has important benefits on the mental and spiritual levels. As we increase our capacity to hold a posture for extended periods of time, not only is our physical strength enhanced but also our psychological endurance and will power are strengthened. Through the cultivation of self-discipline and will power, we are able to assume a posture effortlessly and to hold it without discomfort. This leads to the quality of stillness, when all movement of the body and mind is quieted. As the depth and degree of concentration and relaxation are increased, the breath becomes very subtle. As a result, we can learn to let go of body consciousness and become aware of energy flowing within us. At this point, the mind can be allowed to flow with the breath and a *mantra* can be repeated, with the result that the body, breath, mind, and *mantra* become one. This coordinated effort leads to deeper levels of concentration and meditation.

There are also six cleansings (*kriyas*) that are part of *hatha* yoga practices. These cleansings prepare the body for the postures and like the *asanas*, these *kriyas* have important therapeutic benefits. Some of the *kriyas* also help meditation by enhancing the power of concentration.

Neti (nasal wash) is a simple and frequently used technique where warm salt water is poured into one nostril and allowed to pass out through the other nostril or out the mouth. This cleans out the nose, back of the throat, and sinus cavities and helps in sinusitis, allergies, and upper respiratory infections.

Trataka (gazing) involves focusing the open eyes on an external object such as a candle flame. The eyes can also be directed upwards to stare at the *ajna chakra* (third eye) or downwards at the tip of the nose. This has the effect of improving both eyesight and mental concentration.

Kriyas: Cleansings **
Neti - nasal wash
Trataka - gazing at candle or between eyes
Kapalabhati - breathing technique
Nauli - separation of abdominal muscles
Dhauti - swallowing a cloth
Basti - lower bowel wash
** Practice only under teacher supervision

Kapalabhati, which is also a breathing technique and is described in more detail in chapter 21, *Pranayama* and the Breath, is a vigorous breathing technique that flushes out the respiratory system. It can be used for people who have asthma, sinusitis, and digestive problems.

Nauli is a technique in which the two central abdominal muscles are separated and rolled in a wave-like manner. This promotes better digestion and bowel function. The third *chakra* area is also stimulated and activated by this *kriya*.

Dhauti is an unusual technique practiced only by advanced *hatha* yoga practitioners. A strip of cloth is carefully swallowed and then gently pulled back out to aid in cleansing the throat, esophagus, and stomach.

Basti is another complicated procedure that is used to cleanse the lower colon. The upper wash is yet another type of cleansing that involves swallowing salty or lemon flavored water and then quickly regurgitating the contents of the stomach. This has great therapeutic benefit for stomach problems and asthma.

Examples of Hatha Yoga Asanas

The Spinal Twist

The Bow

The Triangle

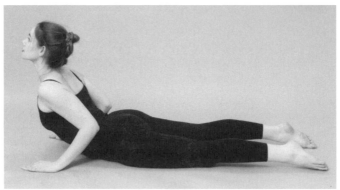

The Child's Pose

The Cobra

Examples of Hatha Yoga Asanas

The Plow

The Bridge

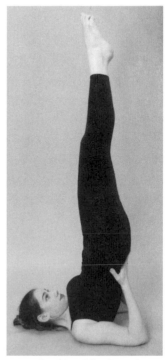

The Shoulder Stand

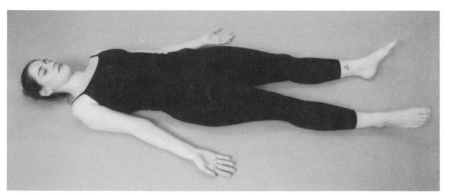

The Corpse

Postures by Aimee McDonald

20. Sitting Postures for Meditation

There are several types of *hatha* yoga postures used in meditation that allow for comfortable sitting. All positions should involve the spine being as straight as possible. The head needs to be in alignment with the chest and torso. The hands are placed on the lap, thighs, or knees and can be placed either face down or upwards. The fingers are situated so that the thumb and index finger of both hands lightly touch each other to form a circle (*mudra*). The eyes are gently closed.

If sitting on a chair, it is best to sit away from the back of the chair so that the spine can be properly aligned. The feet should be placed comfortably on the floor. If sitting against the back of the chair, use a straight back chair with a small pillow placed against the small of the back.

There are five main postures that involve sitting on the floor. Because people raised in the Western world are generally unaccustomed to sitting in this manner, it is recommended that a folded blanket or firm pillow be placed under the hips and buttocks. Three to four inches of elevation will allow for a more upright, steady, and straight spine.

Sukhasana (the easy pose) is the simplest of the cross-legged postures. It causes the least amount of strain on the hips, knees, ankles, and feet. Beginners, people with stiffness in their back or lower extremities, and the elderly often find this position comfortable. Here the right foot is placed below the left knee and the left foot is positioned below the right knee. Each knee then can rest on the opposite foot.

Swastikasana (the auspicious pose) is a bit more complicated cross-legged sitting posture. Here the left leg is bent at the knee and the left foot is placed against the right thigh. The right foot is placed on top of the left calf with the outer edge of the foot and toes tucked in between the thigh and calf muscles. Only the right big toe should be visible here. The toes of the left foot are pulled up between the right thigh and calf, with only the left big toe being visible. The ankle bones and heels are not lined up in this meditation posture.

Siddhasana (the accomplished pose) is a more advanced sitting posture and can be stressful on the lower limbs, especially for beginning students. It is especially helpful when practicing locks (*bandhas*), breath retention (*kumbhaka*), or in attempting to more vigorously activate the latent energy (*kundalini*) of the lower energy center (first *chakra*). Here the root lock is applied by contracting and holding in the anal muscles and the muscles of the perineum. The left heel is placed between the genitals and the anal area. The right heel is placed against the pubic bone above the genitals. The ankle joints are placed so that they are in a line and touch each other. The toes are positioned in the same manner as in the above-mentioned auspicious pose.

Ardha padmasana (the half lotus) is sometimes used in meditation and can be used as a preparation for practicing the full lotus. One foot is placed on the opposite thigh with the heel resting firmly against the abdominal wall. The other leg is bent and tucked comfortably under the top leg.

Padmasana (the lotus pose) is a more strenuous cross-legged sitting pose for meditation. Only people with very flexible ankles and knees can use this position in meditation. The legs are stretched to a great extent and long meditation may become difficult. Because of this stress on the lower extremities, this posture is seldom recommended for meditation. The right foot is placed on the left thigh and the left foot is placed on the right thigh. The heels are placed against the lower abdominal wall.

Common problems that occur while doing the sitting meditation postures are aching or discomfort of the back, hip, knee, or ankle. Paresthesias (pins and needles sensations) of the feet are also a fairly common occurrence. If any of these problems occur, it is often best to gently readjust the position of the back or affected limb and continue meditating.

Sitting Postures for Meditation

Sukhasana, the Easy Sitting Posture

Swastikasana, the Auspicious Posture

Sitting Postures for Meditation

Siddhasana, the Accomplished Posture

Ardha Padmasana, the Half Lotus

Padmasana, the Full Lotus

Photography by Patrick Young

21. *Pranayama* and the Breath

As previously mentioned, *pranayama* is the fourth step in *raja* yoga. In Sanskrit, the word is derived from *prana*, which means "energy" and either *yama*, meaning "control" or *ayama*, which means "expansion." Therefore, the word literally means "a practice in which the flow of energy is expanded and brought under control." *Prana* is further derived from *pra*, which means "first unit" and *na*, meaning "energy." *Prana* refers to the first and the subtlest form of energy, which animates the body and mind as well as the entire universe. All inanimate objects, life forms, and all human sensations, thoughts, feelings, ideas, desires, and knowledge are possible because of *prana*.

While *prana* underlies and sustains all aspects of human functioning, the main vehicle that allows for its control within the body and exchange with the outside world is the breath. This is the reason that breathing techniques are most closely associated with *pranayama*. Although eating also represents a vehicle for exchange of *prana* with the outside world, it occurs only a few times daily, while breathing occurs many times per minute.

The vital importance of breathing is exemplified by the fact that breathing is the first thing we do when we are born and the last thing we do when we die. Even the word for breathing in, inspiration, also means to be motivated or stimulated, while the word for breathing out, exhalation, also means to die. Yogis well disciplined in the science of breath often refer to their age not by the number of years they have been alive but by the number and quality of breaths they have taken.

Breathing is considered to be the link between the conscious and unconscious mind. Unlike heart, kidney, or gastrointestinal functioning, breathing is the only physiologic function that can either be voluntarily controlled by the mind or, if we choose not to pay attention to the flow of the breath, the body can involuntarily and automatically control breathing. Therefore, in the conscious act of doing certain types of breathing exercises, we gain greater awareness and control of involuntary physical functions, as well as the unconscious mind. A more detailed discussion of the close interaction between breathing, the nose, the chest, the autonomic nervous system, the brain, and the mind can be found in chapter 9, Meditation and Its Effects on the Stress Response.

Disruptions in concentration are often associated with pauses and hesitations in breathing. Practicing simple techniques to regulate breathing rhythms brings about greater mental clarity and continuity of thought. Emotional states are often accompanied by altered breathing patterns. Examples of such alterations are the sobbing sounds of grief, the sighs of disappointment, and the trembling breath of anger. Breathing exercises can help regulate these altered patterns of breathing. This results in greater calm and control of emotions.

Breathing exercises can also help quiet and focus the mind to deepen meditation. Meditation can use awareness of the breath flowing in and out of the nose as a focus of concentration. This can be further amplified by simultaneous and silent repetition of certain sounds (*mantras*).

While it usually seems as though we are thinking many things simultaneously, we are in reality instantaneously and rapidly moving from thought to thought. By mentally following the inflow and outflow of the breath, the mind becomes highly focused, does not wander or change, and as a result becomes a more potent tool to appreciate and experience our inner and outer worlds.

The science of breath (*swarodaya*) describes the theory of *prana* and how breathing techniques control the flow and distribution of *prana*. There are several aspects of *pranayama* that are important, including each specific breathing exercise, breath retention (*kumbhaka*), and physical locks (*bandhas*) that are practiced as the student advances. These are all very important exercises for preparing for meditation because they help regulate energy transmission, flow, and distribution of *prana* through the energy pathways (*nadis*) and the main energy centers (*chakras*). Breathing is an invaluable tool in activating the latent spiritual force (*kundalini*) in its ascent to the higher centers of consciousness.

The techniques described below are the most important *pranayama* exercises. Each of these *pranayama* techniques can be practiced using the physical locks and breath retention. This should only be done, however, under the guidance of a teacher who is skilled in the science of breath and who knows the student's general health and formal meditation practice. Except for a few techniques, *pranayama* exercises involve sitting with a straight spine, breathing only through the nose, and allowing the abdomen to move away from the body on inhalation and towards the body on exhalation (diaphragmatic breathing). The rhythm and rate may vary but is generally deep, though not overly forced, and smooth without pauses or jerkiness. If breath retention is not practiced, there should be no hesitation after exhalation or inhalation.

The complete yoga breath involves exaggerating the three phases of breathing in a slow and deep manner. The abdomen slowly moves out on inhalation, followed by rising of the chest, and finishing with the collarbones moving upwards towards the neck. Exhalation follows in the reverse order. This technique is especially helpful when we are tired and want to practice meditation because it brings a great deal of oxygen to the body and feels quite energizing. The complete yoga breath is medically quite helpful for asthma and chronic bronchial conditions, as well as for gastritis and irritable bowel syndrome because of its stimulation of the abdominal muscles and organs.

Nadi shodhanam (alternate nostril breathing) involves alternately breathing through the right and left nostril. After a full and relaxed inhalation through both nostrils, the practitioner uses the tip of the right thumb to block off airflow to the right nostril, and exhales through the left side. This is followed by an inhalation through the left nostril. After slowly taking a full breath, the left nostril is blocked off with the tip of the ring finger and air is eliminated through the right side. After completely exhaling through the right nostril, the breath is drawn in again through the right side. This completes one cycle. The process then repeats itself and three to seven cycles are generally practiced. This technique is generally done before beginning meditation because of its effects on purifying the energy channels (*nadis*) and for the clarity of mind this exercise brings. Alternate nostril breathing has also been shown to be very useful in treating psychological problems such as anxiety, obsessive thought disorders, and depression.

Breathing and Pranayama Techniques
The complete yoga breath - abdomen, chest, and collarbones
Nadi shodhanam - alternate nostril breathing
Ujjayi - sobbing breath
Kapalabhati - shining skull breath
Bhastrika - bellows breath
Bhramari - the bee breath
Sitali - hissing breath
Sitkari - cooling breath
Surya bheda kumbhaka - alternate nostril breathing with retention

Ujjayi (sobbing breath) is a *pranayama* technique practiced by breathing in slowly through both nostrils with the inspired air being felt on the roof of the soft palate. A soft, continuous sobbing sound is made because the glottis remains partially closed. Mental repetition of the *mantra SO* can accompany inhalation. Without any pause, exhalation begins with the out flowing air also being felt on the roof of the mouth. Mentally, the *mantra HAM* (rhythms with the word "rum" and "numb") can be repeated. Seven to twenty-one repetitions can be practiced. *Ujjayi* helps to calm the mind and helps physical conditions such as sore throats, nasal congestion, and sinusitis.

Kapalabhati (shining skull breath) consists of a rapid, vigorous, and forceful expulsion of air using the abdominal muscles and diaphragm. This is followed by a relaxation of the abdominal muscles and a passive, gentle, spontaneous inhalation. Seven to twenty-one repetitions can be done, followed by a brief rest. Three to seven cycles can be practiced. *Kapalabhati* is both a breathing exercise and a *kriya* (cleansing) and is helpful for sinus infections, nasal obstruction, for stimulating the digestive organs, and for exercising the abdominal muscles.

Bhastrika (bellows breath) involves forcefully moving the abdominal muscles in and out so that exhalation and inhalation are vigorous and rapid. One in-and-out breath is one cycle. Between seven and twenty-one cycles are generally practiced and then repeated three to seven times. Alternatively, the practitioner can close off one nostril and do both inhalation and exhalation out of the same side for several repetitions and then switch sides. The benefits of *bhastrika* are similar to *kapalabhati*.

Bhramari (bee breath) is a technique that involves partially closing off the throat and glottis and bringing air in through the nose. A sound is produced on both inhalation and exhalation that resembles the sound of bees in flight. When many people practice this exercise simultaneously it makes a beautiful, melodious sound. This *pranayama* technique can be practiced from seven to twenty-one times. *Bhramari* can be used for thyroid conditions, throat problems, and sinus congestion. It also helps bring about mental clarity before meditation.

Sitali (hissing breath) is practiced by breathing in through the mouth and out through the nose. Two methods of inhalation are possible. The student can turn the tongue backwards so that the tip is resting on the soft palate. Breath is then taken in through the pressure of the combined resistance of the tongue and soft palate. The other, more common approach is to roll the tongue lengthwise into a tube-like structure and protrude the tongue a little beyond the lips. Exhalation in both instances is slowly out through the nose. This *pranayama* technique is useful for cooling the body, which is helpful for conditions that involve excess body heat including fever, menopausal hot flashes, or being overheated from exercise or hot weather.

Sitkari (cooling breath) involves breathing in through the mouth and out through the nose. The teeth are closed and the tongue is placed so that it does not touch the teeth, palate, or bottom of the mouth. Air is drawn in making a loud nose. The breath is deep and slow. Exhalation is done quietly. This can be practiced from seven to twenty-one times. Benefits include cooling the body, helping insomnia, and controlling the appetite.[23]

Surya bheda kumbhaka is another more complex *pranayama* technique. This is discussed in the next chapter, *Kundalini*.

22. *Kundalini*

Kundalini is the subtlest form of *prana* and is often called the primal energy of consciousness. Within the human, *kundalini* is associated with both active (kinetic) and latent (potential) energy. The active form of *kundalini* is used to maintain the mental and physical functioning of the organism. There is also a vast amount of surplus energy not utilized by the mind or body and this is described as being stored as potential energy within the first *chakra*. *Kundalini* is derived from the Sanskrit word, *kundala*, which means "coiled" and it is also associated with the meaning "bowl of fire." The idea of *kundalini* is visualized in meditation as a resting or sleeping serpent that is coiled up, whose inner heat and power are stored as potential energy.

According to Tantra, everything in the cosmos is also found in humans and each person is considered a miniature universe. The latent energy of *kundalini* is not only found in each human being but also in every particle, atom, and molecule in the universe. In most individuals, *kundalini* lies dormant throughout their lifetimes and they are unaware of its existence. The object of meditation in the Tantra and yoga traditions is to awaken, move, and then unite individual *kundalini* with the *kundalini* energy that permeates the larger cosmos. The goal of meditation is to unite the feminine, individual *kundalini* energy called *shakti* located within the first *chakra* with the masculine, universal *kundalini* energy called *shiva* located within the seventh *chakra*, resulting in the birth of the highest state of consciousness. The word yoga means "union," and *kundalini* yoga involves using practices that include meditation and advanced breathing exercises that lead *kundalini* through the *chakra*s and unite it with the pure consciousness associated with the crown *chakra*.

During the process of intense concentration and deep meditation, latent *kundalini* energy stored in the first *chakra* is activated and moved upwards through the central *nadi*, *sushumna*.

Energy is also redirected from the right-sided *pingala* and left *ida* into *sushumna* because the pathway through the central *nadi* to the crown *chakra* is more direct and straightforward.

As the energy rises through the *chakra*s, each center is activated and the physical, mental, and spiritual qualities of each *chakra* are experienced. For example, when the first *chakra* is activated, we will feel grounded and secure. An energized second *chakra* is associated with healthy sexual identity, the third *chakra* with a strong sense of self and ego, the fourth with the ability to love and feel compassion, the fifth with the qualities of communication and creativity, and the sixth with the qualities of intuition and insight. When the seventh and highest *chakra* is pierced and energized, we will experience the highest states of consciousness associated with feelings of union, pure joy, freedom, and inner peace.

There are specific *hatha* yoga and breathing techniques that help stimulate *kundalini* from its latent state. Three physical locks (*bandhas*) force *prana* to move in opposite directions. This creates tension and internal heat, arousing *kundalini* from her quiet slumber.

When practicing *jalandhara bandha* (the chin lock), we swallow first and then place our chin onto the chest. This forces the normally upwards-moving *prana* to move downwards.

When we perform *mula bandha* (the anal lock), we contract the perineum and anal muscles and hold them in this position. This forces the normally downwards-moving *apana* to move upwards.

We apply *uddiyana bandha* (the abdominal lock) by first exhaling and then holding the breath on exhalation. Drawing the abdominal muscles upward towards the spine follows this retention of breath. As the forces of *prana* and *apana* merge, the abdominal lock is used to increase the compression of the energies.

Kumbhaka is a technique of holding the breath either at the end of exhalation or the end of inhalation. When breath holding is practiced at the same time as the three locks, this has the effect of further intensifying the compression. The union of the *pranic* forces created by applying the locks along with breath retention is analogous to a hollow tube that has a piston working at both ends, not allowing any air to escape, with internal heat being created as a result. This heat activates *kundalini* to rise up into *sushumna* on its journey upward to the higher *chakras*.

Agni sara, which means "fanning the fire," is a variation of the abdominal lock and is practiced by first exhaling and then holding the breath on exhalation. After the abdomen is drawn upwards towards the spine, the abdomen is relaxed to move away from the spine and then contracted back again. This is repeated in rapid successions. This has the effect of further heating up the internal *pranic* forces.

Surya bheda kumbhaka is an advanced *pranayama* technique that can also help activate *kundalini*. This breathing technique involves inhaling through the right nostril and at the end of inhalation, applying the chin lock and holding the breath. Before the breath retention becomes uncomfortable, the abdominal and anal locks are also applied for a few seconds. Then the breath is exhaled slowly through the left nostril. Following complete exhalation, inhalation begins and the process is repeated. This process should not be forced, the breath should not be uncomfortable, and repetitions should gradually be increased from a beginning of three. This is a complex technique and should only be done under the guidance of a teacher and after developing a regular meditation practice in which the mind is stable and content.

Shaktipat is a special way that *kundalini* can be activated in a student. This occurs when a teacher, who is advanced in meditation and has learned to concentrate his or her mind and will, transfers energy to the student. This has the effect of catalyzing and rousing the *kundalini* from its dormant state. Only a teacher with pure intentions and heart can practice true *shaktipat* and only a sincere and prepared student can receive it.

During meditation there are various physical and mental changes that may be associated with activation of *kundalini*. True signs are always accompanied by a sense of joy, integration, and increased awareness. Some of these signs are automatic movements of the body into yoga postures and spontaneous occurrences of advanced breathing exercises with breath retention and application of locks. The breathing may stop without any willful effort, neither being in inhalation nor in exhalation. Electrical currents may be felt traveling up the spine. Often the spontaneous reciting of *mantras* or other unusual sounds occur. The eyes may roll upwards or the tongue may curl back towards the throat. Sounds such as bells, drums, or waterfalls may be heard, especially in the right ear. Beautiful and inspiring images may appear in the mind. In deep meditation the lotus petals associated with the different *chakras* are sometimes seen to be hanging downwards, and as the energy rises and activates the center, the lotus-like flowers turn upwards. There may be deep insight into profound or obscure philophies or concepts. There may be momentary feelings that the mind and body dissolve into infinity. During and after these experiences there is no fear and always a sense of awe, peace, and feelings of unity.

On the other hand, there may be no obvious or extraordinary experience at all. Instead, some people experience sudden surges of mental or physical energy, increased enthusiasm, bursts of creativity, peak experiences, or a wonderful sense of well-being. These more subtle experiences are generally accompanied by a slow and gradual evolution of growing wisdom, courage, and patience, and an enhanced ability to be intimate and have compassion for others. The actual experience of *kundalini* activity depends on our personality and on our inner nature. The unfolding of *kundalini* is a reflection of the past patterns of our life and our own *karma*, deeds, and desires.

There is an interesting similarity between the concept of *kundalini*, the *nadis*, and the *chakras* and the symbol often used for the practice of medicine. This symbol is called the caduceus and is found in Greek mythology. It is pictured as two serpents wrapped and intertwined around a central staff, intersecting at several points as they travel upwards. At the top of the staff are two wings. This symbol looks almost identical to the meditative images described above. The staff represents *sushumna* within the spinal cord, the snakes represent *ida* and *pingala* as they criss-cross upwards, the points of intersection represent the *chakras*, and the wings appear like the two lotus petals of the sixth *chakra*. The whole picture represents the path of the *kundalini* as it rises upwards towards the highest stage of consciousness. Since the caduceus represents the symbol for health and healing, its similarity to the traditional imagery associated with meditation reflects the ancient awareness that the ultimate form of health is the spiritual unfolding of consciousness.[24]

Part V

How to Meditate

23. Creating the Environment for Meditation

Try to find a place for meditation that you will use regularly. It should be dry, quiet, and slightly cool. The environment should be free from distractions. Try to face the north or east. Attempt to meditate at the same time each day. Early morning or late at night are particularly quiet times and thus are auspicious for meditating, but if this is not possible, any time is fine.

It is best not to meditate if you are tired or drowsy because sleep is not the goal of meditation. Avoid eating before meditation because meals can also lead to sleepiness. Consider doing yoga postures before meditating to stretch the muscles and strengthen the spine. Practicing alternate nostril breathing and *bhramari* (bee breath) before meditation can also help enhance concentration.

Find a comfortable sitting posture that suits you. Be sure your back is straight. If you choose to sit in a chair, sit so that your feet touch the ground. If you sit on the floor, have a folded blanket under your hips so that your head, trunk, and hips are lined up. Carefully place your feet in a position so they don't fall asleep. You may want to wrap yourself in a blanket or shawl to stay comfortably warm.

You may want to slowly increase the time spent in meditation. Ten to fifteen minutes is a reasonable amount of time to begin with, gradually building up to twenty to sixty minutes. As you gain more experience, you may spend as much time as you want meditating. Be realistic about how much time you have to spend practicing meditation, especially if you have small children to take care of or you are particularly busy at work or school. It is not necessary to change your general habit or activity patterns or adapt a meditative life style. Create an internal state of mind where you look forward to your practice each day. If you miss a day, do not be discouraged. Simply resume your practice the next day.

24. The Technique of Meditation

The form of meditation presented here is based on the philosophies of Tantra, Samkhya, and Vedanta and closely follows the eight steps of *raja* yoga. It is a system practiced for thousands of years in the Himalayan Mountains. First you prepare yourself mentally for the practice by following the life-long goals of *yamas* (regulations) and *niyamas* (observances). Next, you can do *hatha* yoga *asanas* to stretch the back and make the body limber. You then sit with a straight spine in meditation using a *hatha* yoga sitting posture and begin to mentally relax the body. You then practice some simple breathing exercises to begin focusing the mind. More advanced *pranayama* techniques, which include alternate nostril breathing, *bhramari*, and *ujjayi*, can be used to clear the *nadis* and *sushumna*. Sense withdrawal (*pratyahara*) follows as you practice letting go of your thoughts, feelings, and desires and move inwards to the deeper aspects of your mind. Then you begin to concentrate (*dharana*) on a specific object. The objects of concentration used in this form of *raja* yoga-based meditation are *mantras*, *yantras*, *chakras*, light, color, and breath. Concentration on these objects leads to more sustained and intense meditation (*dhyana*) and ultimately to the highest level of consciousness, *samadhi*.

The goal of this meditative practice is to move latent *kundalini* energy, which is stored in the first *chakra*, up through the *chakras* to the higher centers. This is basically done through mental effort and sometimes with the help of more advanced physical practices such as locks and breath retention. An experienced teacher can also help activate *kundalini* in their students through the transfer of highly focused energy (*shaktipat*).

You need not be concerned with results each time you meditate. Because of the sustained mental concentration, the process itself automatically stimulates *kundalini* to ascend upwards. It is not necessary to dwell on the attributes of an individual *chakra* to try to change a particular concern or attitude that might be associated with that center. To specifically activate or stimulate a *chakra*, there are certain other concentration techniques that can be practiced under the guidance of a knowledgeable teacher.

With this form of meditation, you need simply visualize the *chakra* along with awareness of the breath and your *mantra*. At the same time, observe whatever feeling, thought, or sensation may arise and then gently let it go. This meditative technique leads to the slow and steady transformation of physical, psychological, and emotional problems, as well as to the refinement of spiritual qualities and ultimately to the highest states of consciousness.

There will be a growing sense of competence, an inner calmness, and feelings of a stable inner center. Your constant mental activity slows, the mind becomes quieter, and your emotions become steady. Decision-making becomes easier and you become more intuitive and creative. You develop a greater capacity for compassion for others and an increased ability to let go of hurt, resentment, and anxiety. There is a strengthening of the ego and at the same time a sense that you are not defined or restricted by the ego, as you begin to realize you are intimately interconnected with the entire universe around you. As you progress with consistent practice, the inner sounds and vibration of your *mantra* flow effortlessly into your mind, resulting in the experience of greater peace and joy.

****

The following meditation is appropriate for both beginning and more experienced students. Until you feel comfortable meditating and establish a steady and consistent practice, progress slowly through the following seven phases. You may decide to stop at any phase or you may want to work with the more complex practice. At the beginning of each phase is a summary of the preceding phases. This will help you remember the progression of the meditation. Spend two to four weeks on each phase before progressing to the next. The complete meditation is presented in Phase VII. As outlined, become familiar with the geometric form of the *chakra*s before adding color to them. To help you with the visual images of the *chakra*s, refer to the front cover of this book.

Please read through each phase to become familiar with the meditation. Then put the book down and begin. You may also listen to the audio-tapes or audio CD's that accompany this book. These audio guides will lead you through similar phases as outlined below.

The Technique of Meditation
Phase I - Awareness of body and breath
Body posture
Progressive relaxation
Abdominal breathing
Breath awareness
Sense withdrawal
Ending meditation
Phase II - Awareness of the sixth chakra
Phase III - Awareness of the sixth chakra with mantra
Phase IV - Awareness of the seventh chakra
Phase V - Awareness of the first chakra and kundalini
Phase VI - Awareness of all the chakras
Phase VII - Awareness of all the chakras with color: The complete meditation

Phase I: Awareness of Body and Breath

Body Posture

Sit comfortably on a straight-backed chair or on the floor with a firm cushion under you so that your hips are elevated a few inches off the floor. Be sure your back is straight, with your head, chest, and pelvis all in alignment. Your hands are placed comfortably in your lap, thigh, or knees with your palms faced either down or upwards. Touch the tips of your index fingers with the tips of your thumbs, forming a small circle with each hand. Gently close your eyes.

Give yourself permission to let go of thoughts of your daily activities and concerns. Be aware of your body and the space that your body occupies.

Progressive Relaxation

Begin to relax your body. Send warm relaxing energy to each body part. Let all the muscles soften. Begin at the top of your head and move down to your face and relax your eyes, eyelids, mouth, teeth, tongue, lips, jaws, throat, and neck. Let the muscles of your shoulders soften and send warm energy down your arms to your fingers. Move down and relax your chest muscles, heart, and lungs. Then relax the abdominal muscles and the organs inside. Relax your entire back and spine. Then send this relaxing energy to your pelvic area, to your buttocks, and down your legs to your toes.

Abdominal and Diaphragmatic Breathing

Be aware of your breathing. Be sure to breathe quietly through your nose. Breathe deeply, slowly, and evenly without strain. Eliminate any pauses or hesitations while breathing and especially avoid the tendency to pause during the transition between inhalation and exhalation and between exhalation and inhalation. Visualize for a moment a perfectly round circle and imagine that you are inhaling with half the circle and exhaling with the other half.

As you inhale, allow the lower part of the chest and upper part of the abdomen to move out away from the body. Then, as you exhale, allow your abdomen and lower chest to move inwards towards the body. Continue this diaphragmatic breathing for about one minute.

Breath Awareness

Bring your attention to the flow of the breath through your nose. With your mind, follow your breath from the tip of your nose to the point between your two eyebrows as you inhale. Then follow your breath back down again as you exhale. Notice the coolness as the breath flows up the nose on inhalation and the warmth as the breath flows down on exhalation. Continue this breath awareness for a few extra moments.

Sense Withdrawal

Follow your breath up to the area between your two eyebrows and keep your concentration there. Remind yourself that you have a body to use and enjoy the world, that you are a breathing being and your breath connects you to the world, that you have senses to experience the world, and that you have a conscious and unconscious mind to understand the world. But remember that you are also more than all this. For you are both an individual yet part of a larger whole, like a wave that has its own form but is also part of the greater ocean. You are a wave of beauty and a wave of bliss merging with the waves of universal consciousness.

Continue to keep your concentration at the point between your two eyebrows and be aware of the inflow and outflow of your breath for a few more minutes. Watch your thoughts, worries, memories, and feelings float by with simple, neutral, nonjudgmental awareness. Each time your mind is distracted, gently bring your concentration back to this area.

Ending the Meditation

As you slowly come out of the meditation, be aware of your breath flowing through your nostrils for a few moments. Feel the coolness of the breath rising up the nose and the warmth of the breath as it flows back down. Now feel the movement of your abdomen as it moves away from your body as you inhale and back towards your body as you exhale. Finally, be aware of your body and the space that your body occupies. Tell yourself that you will take the same feelings of calm awareness, peace, and joy that you experienced during this meditation back into your everyday life. Slowly bring your hands up to your face, cover your eyes with the center of the palms, and then gently open your eyes. Gently bring your hands down to your lap while continuing to look at the center of the palms. Slowly look up and enjoy the moment.

Phase II: Awareness of the Sixth *Chakra* (Third Eye)

Be aware of your body posture and practice progressive relaxation, abdominal breathing, breath awareness, and sense withdrawal.

With your focus of concentration continuing at the center of your forehead between your eyebrows at the sixth *chakra*, visualize a third eye. This is visualized as a circle with two lotus petals on both sides. This is the center of insight, intuition, and wisdom. This eye sees inwards, watching your thoughts, worries, memories, and feelings float by. It is accompanied by simple, neutral, nonjudgmental awareness. Gently bring your concentration back to the image of the third eye each time your mind is distracted.

Allow your attention to remain at the center of the third *chakra*, visualizing the third eye, for the rest of the meditation and for as long as you wish.

****

As you slowly come out of the meditation, be aware of your breath flowing through your nostrils for a few moments. Feel the coolness of the breath rising up the nose and the warmth of the breath as it flows back down. Now feel the movement of your abdomen as it moves away from your body as you inhale and back towards your body as you exhale. Finally, be aware of your body and the space that your body occupies. Tell yourself that you will take the same feelings of calm awareness, peace, and joy that you experienced during this meditation back into your everyday life. Slowly bring your hands up to your face, cover your eyes with the center of the palms, and then gently open your eyes. Gently bring your hands down to your lap while continuing to look at the center of the palms. Slowly look up and enjoy the moment.

Phase III: Awareness of the Sixth *Chakra* with *Mantra*

Be aware of your body posture and practice progressive re-laxation, abdominal breathing, breath awareness, and sense withdrawal. Be aware of the third eye.

Begin to mentally repeat the sound of your *mantra*. You can use one of three different *mantras*: the *mantra OM*, the *mantra SO HAM*, or a personal *mantra* if you were given one by your meditation teacher. You may want to coordinate your *mantra* with your breathing. You can repeat your *mantra* with each separate inhalation and exhalation, with one round of breathing that includes one inhalation and exhalation, or with several rounds. If you seem to hear the *mantra* resonating deep within, you may also simply listen to the inner sound and vibration of the *mantra*.

Allow your attention to remain at this center of the third eye, listening to the *mantra* for the rest of the meditation and for as long as you wish.

****

As you slowly come out of the meditation, be aware of your breath flowing through your nostrils for a few moments. Feel the coolness of the breath rising up the nose and the warmth of the breath as it flows back down. Now feel the movement of your abdomen as it moves away from your body as you inhale and back towards your body as you exhale. Finally, be aware of your body and the space that your body occupies. Tell yourself that you will take the same feelings of calm awareness, peace, and joy that you experienced during this meditation back into your everyday life. Slowly bring your hands up to your face, cover your eyes with the center of the palms, and then gently open your eyes. Gently bring your hands down to your lap while continuing to look at the center of the palms. Slowly look up and enjoy the moment.

Phase IV: Awareness of the Seventh *Chakra* (Crown *Chakra*)

Be aware of your body posture and practice progressive re-laxation, abdominal breathing, breath awareness, and sense withdrawal. Be aware of the third eye. Be aware of the third eye and mentally repeat or listen for the mantra OM, SO HAM, or your personal mantra.

As you inhale, follow your breath, mind, and *mantra* upwards and bring your concentration to the seventh *chakra* at the top part of your brain (cerebral cortex). Visualize a lotus flower with a thousand petals emanating light upwards above your head. Imagine your individual self-identity and the entire field of universal consciousness blending into one indissoluble whole. Keep your focus here for one to five minutes.

Let your concentration gently move back to the sixth *chakra* (third eye). Allow your attention to remain at this center, listening to the *mantra*, for the rest of the meditation and for as long as you wish.

****

As you slowly come out of the meditation, be aware of your breath flowing through your nostrils for a few moments. Feel the coolness of the breath rising up the nose and the warmth of the breath as it flows back down. Now feel the movement of your abdomen as it moves away from your body as you inhale and back towards your body as you exhale. Finally, be aware of your body and the space that your body occupies. Tell yourself that you will take the same feelings of calm awareness, peace, and joy that you experienced during this meditation back into your everyday life. Slowly bring your hands up to your face, cover your eyes with the center of the palms, and then gently open your eyes. Gently bring your hands down to your lap while continuing to look at the center of the palms. Slowly look up and enjoy the moment.

Phase V: Awareness of the First *Chakra* and *Kundalini*

Be aware of your body posture and practice progressive relaxation, abdominal breathing, breath awareness, and sense withdrawal. Be aware of the third eye. Be aware of the third eye and mentally repeat or listen for the mantra OM, SO HAM, or your personal mantra. Be aware of the seventh chakra.

As you exhale, follow your breath, mind, and *mantra* down the center of the spine to the first *chakra*, located across from the perineum, at the base of the spine near the tailbone. Visualize an inverted, downward-directed triangle located inside a circle. In the center of the triangle, concentrate on the great amount of latent energy (*kundalini*) stored there. This is visualized as an awakening serpent that is coiled around itself three and one-half times with its head facing upwards. Experience the feelings of being grounded, the sense of physical and emotional stability, and the inner security associated with this center.

While listening to the *mantra*, feel the energy slowly moving upwards through the spine to the top of your head as you inhale and follow the energy back down the spine to the first *chakra* as you exhale. You may continue this awareness of energy movement for as long as you wish.

****

As you slowly come out of the meditation, be aware of your breath flowing through your nostrils for a few moments. Feel the coolness of the breath rising up the nose and the warmth of the breath as it flows back down. Now feel the movement of your abdomen as it moves away from your body as you inhale and back towards your body as you exhale. Finally, be aware of your body and the space that your body occupies. Tell yourself that you will take the same feelings of calm awareness, peace, and joy that you experienced during this meditation back into your everyday life. Slowly bring your hands up to your face, cover your eyes with the center of the palms, and then gently open your eyes. Gently bring your hands down to your lap while continuing to look at the center of the palms. Slowly look up and enjoy the moment.

Phase VI: Awareness of All the *Chakras*

Be aware of your body posture and practice progressive relaxation, abdominal breathing, breath awareness, and sense withdrawal. Be aware of the third eye. Be aware of the third eye and mentally repeat or listen for the mantra OM, SO HAM, or your personal mantra. Be aware of the seventh chakra. Be aware of the first chakra and kundalini.

As you inhale, follow your breath, mind, and *mantra* up to the second *chakra* located within the spinal cord. This center is directly opposite and slightly above the genital region. Visualize a crescent moon within a circle. Feel the balance of masculine and feminine qualities within and the inner strength to appropriately direct sensual and sexual energies. Continue to concentrate on this *chakra* from one to five minutes.

As you inhale, follow your breath, mind, and *mantra* up to the third *chakra* located across from the navel within the spinal cord. Visualize an upward facing triangle inside a circle. Feel the heat and power here, as the rising energy is amplified and concentrated at this important transforming energy center. Experience your individuality and the strength of your own ego. Continue this concentration from one to five minutes.

As you inhale, follow your breath, mind, and *mantra* up to the fourth *chakra* located across from the heart within the spine. Visualize two intersecting triangles (Star of David) inside a circle. In the center of the triangles, visualize yourself sitting in a meditative posture in a dark cave looking at a flame from a candle that does not flicker. This light is described as being the reflection of the soul. Feel the calmness, sense of love, and compassion associated with this center. Remain at this center from one to five minutes.

As you inhale, follow your breath, mind, and *mantra* up to the fifth *chakra* across from the throat within the spine. Visualize a full moon on a sky inside a circle. Experience feelings of being nurtured by the higher consciousness that lies within. Feel your openness to accept creative impulses from an inner, unlimited source. Continue this focus from one to five minutes. If you tend to be a creative, artistic, or musically talented person, you may want to spend extra time at this center of consciousness.

As you inhale, follow your breath, mind, and *mantra* up to the sixth *chakra*. Visualize the third eye being across from the center of the eyebrows in the deeper part of the middle brain. Experience the inner vision, insight, and intuitive knowledge associated with this center. Allow the focus to remain here from one to five minutes.

As you inhale, follow your breath, mind, and *mantra* up to the crown *chakra* located deep within the cortex of the brain. Again visualize light from a thousand lotus petals shining brightly. Imagine your individual self-identity and the entire field of universal consciousness blending into one indissoluble whole. Continue this visualization from one to five minutes.

As you exhale, follow your breath, mind, and *mantra* back to the third eye. Allow your attention to remain at this center, listening to the *mantra*, for the rest of the meditation and for as long as you wish. (You may also maintain your concentration on the heart or throat center. The *chakra* you remain at for the rest of the meditation depends on instructions from your teacher and upon your own personality, emotional needs, or spiritual strengths.)

****

As you slowly come out of the meditation, be aware of your breath flowing through your nostrils for a few moments. Feel the coolness of the breath rising up the nose and the warmth of the breath as it flows back down. Now feel the movement of your abdomen as it moves away from your body as you inhale and back towards your body as you exhale. Finally, be aware of your body and the space that your body occupies. Tell yourself that you will take the same feelings of calm awareness, peace, and joy that you experienced during this meditation back into your everyday life. Slowly bring your hands up to your face, cover your eyes with the center of the palms, and then gently open your eyes. Gently bring your hands down to your lap while continuing to look at the center of the palms. Slowly look up and enjoy the moment.

Phase VII: Awareness of All *Chakra* Colors: The Complete Meditation

Sit comfortably on a straight-backed chair or on the floor with a firm cushion under you so that your hips are elevated a few inches off the floor. Be sure your back is straight, with your head, chest and pelvis all in alignment. Your hands are placed comfortably on your lap, thighs, or knees with the palms faced either down or upwards. Touch the tips of your index fingers with the tips of your thumbs, forming a small circle with each hand. Gently close your eyes.

Give yourself permission to let go of thoughts of your daily activities and concerns. Be aware of your body and the space that your body occupies.

Begin to relax your body. Send warm relaxing energy to each body part. Let all the muscles soften. Begin at the top of your head and move down to your face and relax your eyes, eyelids, mouth, teeth, tongue, lips, jaw, throat, and neck. Let the muscles of your shoulders soften and send warm energy down your arms to your fingers. Move down and relax your chest muscles, heart, and lungs. Then relax the abdominal muscles and the organs inside. Relax your entire back and spine. Then send this relaxing energy to your pelvic area, to your buttocks, and down your legs to your toes.

Be aware of your breathing. Be sure to breathe quietly through your nose. Breathe deeply, slowly, and evenly, without strain. Eliminate any pauses or hesitations while breathing and especially avoid the tendency to pause during the transition between inhalation and exhalation and between exhalation and inhalation. Visualize for a moment a perfectly round circle and imagine that you are inhaling with half the circle and exhaling with the other half.

As you inhale, allow the lower part of the chest and upper part of the abdomen to move out away from the body. Then as you exhale, allow the abdomen and lower chest to move inwards towards the body. Continue this diaphragmatic breathing for about one minute.

Bring your attention to the flow of the breath through your nose. With your mind, follow your breath from the tip of your nose to the point between your two eyebrows as you inhale. Then follow your breath back down again as you exhale. Notice the coolness as the breath flows up the nose on inhalation and the warmth as the breath flows down on exhalation. Continue this breath awareness for a few extra moments.

Follow your breath up to the area between your two eyebrows and keep your concentration there. Remind yourself that you have a body to use and enjoy the world, that you are a breathing being and your breath connects you to the world, that you have senses to experience the world, and that you have a conscious and unconscious mind to understand the world. But remember that you are also more than all this. You are both an individual yet part of a larger whole, like a wave that has its own form but is also part of the greater ocean. You are a wave of beauty and a wave of bliss merging with the waves of universal consciousness.

With your focus of concentration continuing at the center of your forehead between your eyebrows (sixth *chakra*), visualize a third eye, seen as a white circle with two light blue lotus petals on the sides. Inside the circle is a small white inverted triangle. This is the center of insight, intuition, and wisdom. This eye sees inwards, watching your thoughts, worries, memories, and feelings float by. It is accompanied by simple, neutral, nonjudgmental awareness. Each time your mind is distracted, gently bring your concentration back to the image of the third eye.

Begin to mentally repeat the sound of your *mantra*. You can use one of three different *mantras*: the *mantra OM*, the *mantra SO HAM*, or a personal *mantra* if you have been given one by your meditation teacher. You may want to coordinate your *mantra* with your breathing. You can repeat your *mantra* with each separate inhalation and exhalation, with one cycle of breathing that includes one inhalation and exhalation, or with several cycles. If you seem to hear the *mantra* resonating deep within, you may also simply listen to the inner sound and vibration of the *mantra*.

As you inhale, follow your breath, mind, and *mantra* upwards and bring your concentration to the top part of your brain, the cerebral cortex. Visualize a lotus flower with a thousand petals emanating either white light or light the color of the rainbow, four inches above your head. Imagine your individual self-identity and the entire field of universal consciousness blending into one indissoluble whole. Keep your focus here from one to five minutes.

As you exhale, follow the breath, mind, and *mantra* down the center of the spine to the first *chakra*, located across from the perineum, at the base of the spine near the tailbone. Visualize a red inverted, downward-directed equilateral triangle surrounded by a yellow square, both shapes resting inside a circle. Resting on the circle are four red lotus petals. In the center of the triangle, concentrate on the great amount of latent energy (*kundalini*) stored there. This is visualized as an awakening serpent that is coiled around itself three and one-half times with its head facing upwards. Experience the feelings of being grounded, the sense of physical and emotional stability, and the inner security associated with this center. Feel the energy slowly moving upwards through the spine from one to five minutes.

As you inhale, follow your breath, mind, and *mantra* up to the second *chakra* located within the spinal cord. This center is directly opposite and slightly above the genital region. Visualize a silver-white crescent moon within a circle. Resting on the circle are six dark red lotus petals. Feel the balance of masculine and feminine qualities within and the inner strength to appropriately direct sensual and sexual energies. Continue to concentrate on this *chakra* from one to five minutes.

As you inhale, follow your breath, mind, and *mantra* up to the third *chakra* located across from the navel within the spinal cord. Visualize a dark red, upward facing triangle inside a circle. Resting on the circle are ten dark blue lotus petals. Feel the great heat and power here, as the rising energy is amplified and concentrated at this important transforming energy center. Experience your individuality and the strength of your own ego. Continue this concentration from one to five minutes.

As you inhale, follow your breath, mind, and *mantra* up to the fourth *chakra* located across the heart within the spine. Visualize two intersecting triangles (Star of David) that are a blue-green color inside a circle. Resting on the circle are twelve dark red lotus petals. In the center of the triangles, visualize yourself sitting in a meditative posture in a dark cave looking at a flame from a candle that does not flicker. This light is described as being the reflection of the soul. Feel the calmness, sense of love, and compassion associated with this center. Remain at this center from one to five minutes.

As you inhale, follow your breath, mind, and *mantra* up to the fifth *chakra* across from the throat within the spine. Visualize a white full moon resting within a white triangle. This image is seen against the background of a deep blue sky. A circle surrounds this and resting on the circle are sixteen purple lotus petals. Experience feelings of being nurtured by the higher consciousness that lies within. Feel your openness to accept creative impulses from an inner, unlimited source. Continue this focus from one to five minutes. If you tend to be a creative, artistic, or musically talented person, you may want to spend extra time at this center of consciousness.

As you inhale, follow your breath, mind, and *mantra* up to the sixth *chakra*, which is visualized as a white circle with two medium blue lotus petals on the sides. Inside the circle is a small, white triangle that is pointed downwards. Visualize the third eye being across from the center of the eyebrows in the deeper part of the middle brain. Experience the inner vision, insight, and intuitive knowledge associated with this center. Allow the focus to remain here from one to five minutes.

As you inhale, follow your breath, mind, and *mantra* to the crown *chakra*, located deep within the cortex of the brain. Again visualize white light or light the color of the rainbow emanating from a thousand lotus petals shining brightly upwards. Imagine your individual self-identity and the entire field of universal consciousness blending into one indissoluble whole. Continue this visualization from one to five minutes.

As you exhale, follow your breath, mind, and *mantra* back to the third eye. Allow your attention to remain at this center, listening to your *mantra*, for the rest of the meditation and for as long as you wish. (You may also maintain your concentration on the heart or throat center. The *chakra* where you remain for the rest of the meditation depends on instructions from your teacher and upon your individual personality traits, emotional needs, and spiritual strengths.)

****

As you slowly come out of the meditation, be aware of your breath flowing through your nostrils for a few moments. Feel the coolness of the breath rising up the nose and the warmth of the breath as it flows back down. Now feel the movement of your abdomen as it moves away from your body as you inhale and back towards your body as you exhale. Finally, be aware of your body and the space that your body occupies. Tell yourself that you will take the same feelings of calm awareness, peace, and joy that you experienced during this meditation back into your everyday life. Slowly bring your hands up to your face, cover your eyes with the center of the palms, and then gently open your eyes. Gently bring your hands down to your lap while continuing to look at the center of the palms. Slowly look up and enjoy the moment.

25. Advanced Meditation Techniques

As you advance in your practice, attempt to spend longer periods in meditation. There are also several techniques that can be incorporated into your practice which can deepen your meditation. These more advanced techniques are directed at intensification of the previously described meditation. Some of these techniques help to activate *kundalini* directly. This is particularly true when you apply the locks and practice breath retention. These latter physical techniques should be undertaken with caution because they tend to amplify and exaggerate physical, emotional, and spiritual concerns that you may be experiencing at the time.

Advice from your meditation teacher can be an invaluable help in deciding whether to make your practice more complex. If you have a strong inclination or intuition to attempt a new technique, try it slowly and methodically. Experiences in your own meditation can sometimes lead you to the next level and practice of meditation. This may occur if you spontaneously hear an inner sound or *mantra*, visualize a specific image or *yantra*, or automatically begin to practice certain advanced breathing techniques or yoga practices.

Following are five examples of more advanced meditation techniques. You should be very familiar with the entire meditation outlined in the previous chapter before you consider practicing these more advanced techniques. Before trying these practices in any specific meditation session, be sure that have carefully and gradually completed all phases of the above-mentioned meditation. It is best to work closely with a meditation teacher who is skilled in these types of practices and who can discuss the wisdom of your doing these more advanced meditation techniques.

1. Repeat the *bija mantra* as you concentrate on each *chakra*. As you ascend through each *chakra*, mentally repeat the following *mantras*: *LAM* at the first *chakra*, *VAM* at the second

chakra, *RAM* at the third *chakra*, *YAM* at the fourth *chakra*, *HAM* at the fifth *chakra*, and *OM* at the sixth *chakra*.

2. After moving through all the *chakras* described in the complete meditation and having concentrated on the sixth *chakra* for some time, slowly let all inner visualizations disappear. Simply be present. Experience the *mantra* and the sounds of silence within. Continue this for as long as you wish.

3. After moving through all the *chakras* described in the complete meditation, bring your final concentration point to the *guru chakra*, located within the brain between the sixth and seventh *chakra*s. This lesser known *chakra* is an extremely subtle center associated with experiences of fine vibrations, sublime mental images, and feelings of bliss.

4. After practicing the complete meditation, visualize the entire universe and all of its creation dissolving into light. Breathe in this light and imagine the light dissolving into you. Visualize yourself dissolving from above and below simultaneously, with only the clear light of the flame in the center of the heart *chakra* remaining. This is the reflection of the soul, that part of you which is constant and never changing.

5. After practicing the complete meditation, visualize a tiny transparent pearl of pure crystal at the sixth *chakra*. When the vision of this is totally clear, imagine yourself looking deeply through this pearl of pure, colorless light, with the transparency extending to infinity. Move this image to the crown *chakra*. Hold on to this perception of clear light and emptiness with single-pointed concentration. Realize that this infinite empty space has no category of the mind into which it can be placed. This is the experience of the void and the state of nothingness. It is in this state of total emptiness where you are most sensitive, open, and receptive and where you can then be filled with the higher knowledge of universal consciousness.

Endnotes

1. Rama, Swami. *Path of Fire and Light: Advanced Practices of Yoga.* Honesdale, Penn.: Himalayan Institute Press, 1986. 114-116.

2. Ajaya, Swami. *Yoga Psychology: A Practical Guide to Meditation.* Honesdale, Penn.: Himalayan Institute Press, 1976. 6-7.

3. Ibid., 80-86.

4. Suzuki, Shunryu. *Zen Mind, Beginner's Mind.* New York: Weatherhill, 1974. 21-22.

5. Ajaya, *Yoga Psychology*, 16-18.

6. Kaplan, Aryeh. *Jewish Meditation.* New York: Schocken Books, 1985. 35-36.

7. Chernin, Dennis, and Greg Manteuffel. *Health: A Holistic Approach.* Wheaton, Ill.: Quest Books, 1984. 84-99.

8. Goldstein, J., and J. Kornfield. *Seeking the Heart of Wisdom: The Path of Insight Meditation.* Boston, Mass.: Shambhala, 1987. 61-77.

9. Austin, J. *Zen and the Brain.* Cambridge, Mass.: MIT, 1998. 57-148. And Freeman, L., and G. F. Lawlis. *Complementary & Alternative Medicine.* St. Louis, Mo.: Mosby, 2001. 166-196.

10. Chernin and Manteuffel, *Health*, 99-118.

11. Ibid., 99-118.

12. Rama, S., R. Ballentine, and S. Ajaya. *Yoga and Psychotherapy*. Glenview, Ill.: Himalayan Institute Press, 1976. 69-100.

13. Rama, Swami. *Lectures on Yoga*. Honesdale, Penn.: Himalayan Institute Press, 1976. 16-21.

14. Rama, S., R. Ballentine, and A. Hymes. *The Science of Breath*. Honesdale, Penn.: Himalayan Institute Press, 1998. 72-112. And Avalon, Arthur. *The Serpent Power: The Secret of Tantric and Shaktic Yoga*. New York: Dover Publications, 1974. 257-498.

15. Johari, Harish. *Chakras*. Rochester, Vt.: Destiny Books, 1987. 47-84. And Goswami, S. *Layayoga: The Definitive Guide to the Chakras and Kundalini*. Rochester, Vt.: Inner Traditions, 1999. 143-286.

16. Ajaya. *Yoga Psychology*, 53-68.

17. Khanna, Madhu. *Yantra: The Tantric Symbol of Cosmic Unity*. London, England: Thames and Hudson, 1994. 109-130.

18. Pandit, M. P. *Kundalini Yoga*. Pomona, Calif.: Auromere Publications, 1979. 50-60.

19. Kaplan, *Jewish Meditation*, 73-82.

20. Khanna, *Yantra*, 109-130. And Rama, Swami. *Choosing a Path*. Honesdale, Penn.: Himalayan Institute Press, 1988. 187-194.

21. Chernin and Manteuffel, *Health*, 162-176.

22. Rama, Ballentine, and Ajaya, *Yoga and Psychotherapy*, xxiii-xxvii.

23. Rama, *Path of Fire and Light*, 16-21. And

Van Lysbeth, A. *Pranayama*. London, England: Mandala Books, 1979. 140-178.

And Sivananda, Swami. *The Science of Pranayama*. Garhwal, India: The Divine

Life Society, 1971. 74-84.

24. Mookerjee, Ajit. *Kundalini*. Rochester, Vt: Destiny Books, 1986. 71-83. And

Pandit. *Kundalini Yoga*, 50-60. And Tirtha, Swami Vishnu. *Devatma Shakti*.

Delhi, India: Swami Shivan Tirth Publications, 1962. 76-78. And Rama, *Path of

Fire and Light*, 134-144.

Bibliography

Ajaya, Swami. *Yoga Psychology: A Practical Guide to Meditation.* Honesdale, Penn.: Himalayan Institute Press, 1976.

---. *Psychotherapy East and West.* Honesdale, Penn.: Himalayan Institute Press, 1983.

Austin, James. *Zen and the Brain: Towards an Understanding of Meditation and Consciousness.* Cambridge, Mass.: MIT, 1998.

Avalon, Arthur. *The Serpent Power: The Secret of Tantric and Shaktic Yoga.* New York: Dover Publications, 1974.

Chernin, Dennis, and Greg Manteuffel. *Health: A Holistic Approach.* Wheaton, Ill.: Quest Books, 1984.

Digambayi, Swami. *Hathapradipika.* Dehli, India: Kaivalyadhama, 1970.

Eliade, Mircea. *Yoga: Immortality and Freedom.* Princeton, N.J.: Princeton University Press, 1969.

Feurerstein, Greg. *Tantra: The Path of Ecstasy.* Boston, Mass.: Shambhala, 1998.

Freeman, L., and G.F. Lawlis. *Complementary & Alternative Medicine.* St. Louis, Mo.: Mosby, 2001.

Goldstein, J., and Jack Kornfield. *Seeking the Heart of Wisdom: The Path of Insight Meditation.* Boston, Mass.: Shambhala, 1987.

Goswami, S. *Layayoga: The Definitive Guide to the Chakras and Kundalini.* Rochester, Vt.: Inner Traditions, 1999.

Govinda, Lama. *Foundations of Tibetian Mysticism.* York Beach, Me.: Samuel Weiser, 1969.

Iyengar, B. K. S. *Light on Yoga.* New York: Schocken Books, 1975.

Johari, Harish. *Chakras*. Rochester, Vt.: Destiny Books, 1987.

Judith, Anadea. *Eastern Body Western Mind: Psychology and the Chakra System*. Berkeley, Calif.: Celestial Arts, 1996.

Kabat-Zinn, Jon. *Wherever You Go There You Are*. New York: Hyperion, 1994.

Kaplan, Aryeh. *Jewish Meditation*. New York: Schoken Books, 1985.

Khalsa, D., et al. Randomized Controlled Trial of Yogic Meditation Techniques for Patients with Obsessive-Compulsive Disorder. *CNS Spectrums* 4.4 (1999): 34-47.

Khanna, Madhu. *Yantra: The Tantric Symbol of Cosmic Unity*. London: Thames and Hudson, 1994.

Kornfield, Jack. *After the Ecstasy, the Laundry*. New York, N.Y.: Bantam Books, 2000.

LeShan, Lawrence. *How to Meditate*. Boston, Mass.: Back Bay Books, 1999.

Mookerjee, Ajit. *Kundalini*. Rochester, Vt: Destiny Books, 1986.

Pandit, M. P. *Kundalini Yoga*. Pomona, Calif.: Auromere Publications, 1979.

Prabhavananda, S., and C. Isherwood. *How to Know God: The Yoga Aphorisms of Patanjali*. New York: Mentor Books, 1969.

Rama, Swami. *Choosing a Path*. Honesdale, Penn.: Himalayan Institute Press, 1988.

---. *Lectures on Yoga*. Honesdale, Penn.: Himalayan Institute Press, 1976.

---. *Path of Fire and Light: Advanced Practices of Yoga*. Honesdale, Penn.: Himalayan Institute Press, 1986.

Rama, S., R. Ballentine., and S. Ajaya. *Yoga and Psychotherapy*. Glenview, Ill.: Himalayan Institute Press, 1976.

Rama, S., R. Ballentine., and A. Hymes. *The Science of Breath*. Honesdale, Penn.: Himalayan Institute Press, 1998.

Saraswati, Swami. *Asana Pranayama Mudra Bandha*. Bihar, India: Bihar School of Yoga, 1977.

Sivananda, Swami. *The Science of Pranayama*. Garhwal, India: The Divine Life Society, 1971.

Suzuki, Shunryu. *Zen Mind, Beginner's Mind*. New York: Weatherhill, 1974.

Tigunat, Rajmani. *The Path of Mantra and the Mystery of Initiation*. Honesdale, Penn.: Himalayan Institute Press, 1996.

Tirtha, Swami Vishnu. *Devatma Shakti*. Delhi, India: Swami Shivan Tirth Publications, 1962.

Van Lysbeth, A. *Pranayama*. London, England: Mandala Books, 1979.

White, John. *The Highest State of Consciousness*. New York: Doubleday, 1972.

Index